Everyday Home Improvements
Volume I

Complete Handyman's Library™
Handyman Club of America
Minneapolis, Minnesota

Published in 1994 by
Handyman Club of America
12301 Whitewater Drive
Minnetonka, Minnesota 55343

Published by arrangement with Cy DeCosse Incorporated
ISBN 0-86573-741-X

Printed on American paper by
R. R. Donnelley & Sons Co. (0894)

CREDITS:
Created by: The Editors of Cy DeCosse Incorporated in
cooperation with Black & Decker. **BLACK**&**DECKER**
is a trademark of Black & Decker (US), Incorporated and is
used under license.

Contents

Introduction

If your home is like most others, there are a number of small repairs needed throughout the house. Perhaps a broken window in the garage, a small hole in a wall in the kids' playroom, a torn screen on the porch, damaged wallpaper and stains on a kitchen wall...more than enough for you to wish you had help in getting the work done.

Everyday Home Improvements: Volume I provides you with the help you need. It supplies all the information you need to make many common home repairs. You'll learn about all the tools, materials and techniques necessary for each repair project.

First, we show you the essential tools you should have available, including the information you need to make the appropriate choices when purchasing or renting these tools. Everything you need to know about materials such as lumber, sheet goods and fasteners is also shown. You see how to set up an efficient workshop area for your projects, that will also make storing and organizing your tools and materials a snap. You learn about safety issues that will help you work without injury. Plus, you are given plans for building two essentials for your shop, a sturdy workbench and sawhorse.

Then we present all you need to know about repairing windows and doors. Whether you are replacing weatherstripping, glass or screens; repairing latches or locksets; freeing stuck windows or sticking doors or installing a new door, you'll find all the information you need—including any specialty tools to make the job easier.

Next up: walls and ceilings. You learn about working with plaster and wallboard surfaces, fixing everything from cracks to large holes. You see how to deal with stains, mildew and peeling paint. You're shown professional techniques for installing wallboard for large repairs, including taping and sanding, and repair methods for wallcoverings and ceramic tile.

This is followed by floor repairs. You learn to fix damaged carpeting, sheet vinyl, vinyl tile and

hardwood flooring with the information provided. In addition, you see a variety of techniques for dealing with squeaking floors and stairs.

Finally, we take you outside to show you how to fix your leaky roof and damaged shingles, repair gutters and downspouts, fill holes and cracks in cement and asphalt and repair or replace portions of your deck or other wood surfaces. You see which products will do the best repair job for your particular problem.

So keep *Everyday Home Improvements: Volume I* open as you work on your repair projects. You'll find it will help you do professional quality work and make successful repairs every time.

Tools & Materials

A Basic Tool Kit

A medium-sized toolbox with the hand tools shown below will prepare you for most of the home repairs in this book. Whether you buy tools as you need them, or purchase them all at once, always buy the best tools you can afford. A quality hand tool can last a lifetime, and in the long run costs less than three or four cheaper replacements. Select hammers, chisels and screwdrivers that are made of drop-forged steel. Quality hand saws feature precision-ground teeth. A basic tool kit should include: pliers, tape measure, pry bar, open-end wrenches, compact hand saw, hacksaw, combination square, pipe wrench, channel-type pliers, putty knife, adjustable wrench, claw hammer, wood chisel, metal file, sanding block, needlenose pliers, screwdrivers, awl.

Tape measure

Pliers

Pry bar

Compact hand saw

Hacksaw

Open-end wrenches

Pipe wrench

Combination square

Channel-type pliers

Putty knife

Wood chisel

Metal file

Adjustable wrench

Sanding block

Awl

Needlenose pliers

Hammer

Screwdrivers

Basic Power Tools

A few good-quality power tools can greatly expand your skills and level of satisfaction for home repair projects. Any project is faster and easier if you use a power tool. A ⅜" variable-speed reversible drill is one of the most versatile tools you can own: it can drill holes, screw in fasteners, file metal, strip rust and paint — even stir paint. A power jig saw with a variety of blades tackles just about any cutting job. A quality jig saw handles wood stock up to 2" thick. A circular saw with a blade diameter of 7" or more is an essential tool for carpentry projects. A pad sander simplifies wood refinishing jobs.

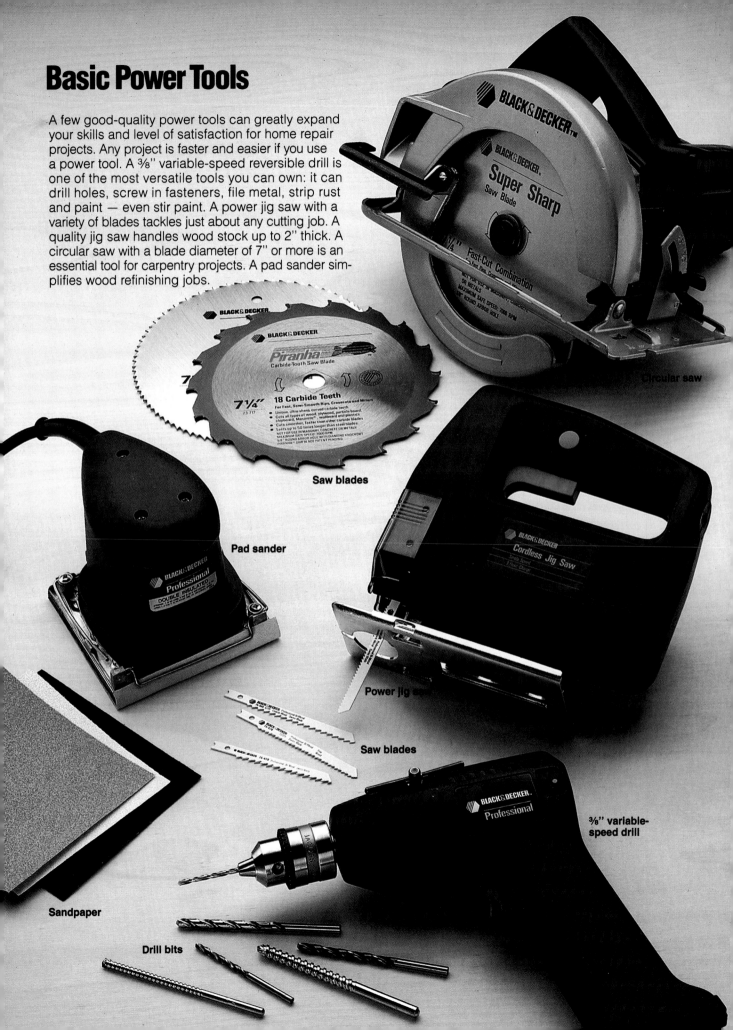

Circular saw

Saw blades

Pad sander

Power jig saw

Saw blades

⅜" variable-speed drill

Sandpaper

Drill bits

Measuring & Layout Tools

An important first step in every carpentry project is measuring distances and angles accurately. Buy a steel tape measure with a ¾-inch-wide blade for general home use.

A combination square is a compact tool used to measure and mark 45° and 90° angles. Use a framing square to lay out 90° angles. Choose a T-bevel with a locking handle to measure and transfer any angle.

To check surfaces for plumb and level, buy a quality 2-foot carpenter's level made of metal or wood. Select a level with screw-in bubble vials that can be replaced if they are damaged. Also buy a string chalk line to lay out long, straight lines.

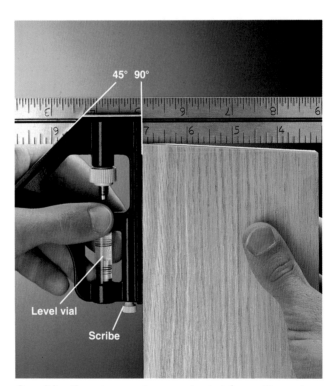

Steel tape measure with ¾-inch-wide blade is good for general-purpose home use. Choose a tape with blade marked every 16″ for easy layout of stud or joist locations.

Combination square is many tools in one. The adjustable handle has two straight surfaces for marking 90° and 45° angles. The square also has a built-in level. Some squares include a pointed metal scribe to mark work for cutting.

Level vial

Scribe

Hammers

Hammers are made in a wide variety of sizes and shapes. Choose a hammer with a smoothly finished, high-carbon steel head and a quality handle made of hickory, fiberglass, or solid steel.

The 16-ounce curved claw hammer is the most frequently used hammer for carpentry. It is designed only for driving, setting, or pulling nails. For all other striking jobs, use a specialty hammer. A tack hammer with a magnetic head drives nails and tacks that are too small to hold. A rubber- or plastic-head mallet drives wood chisels. Select a ball peen hammer to pound hardened metal tools, like masonry chisels or pry bars, because it has a heat-treated steel head that resists chipping.

Use a nail set to drive nail heads below the work surface without damaging the wood.

Tack hammer

Rubber-head mallet

Ball peen hammer

Claw hammer

Nail set

Clean hammer face periodically with fine sandpaper. Wood resins and nail coatings may build up on the face, causing the hammer to slip and mar the work surface or bend the nail.

Hammering Tips

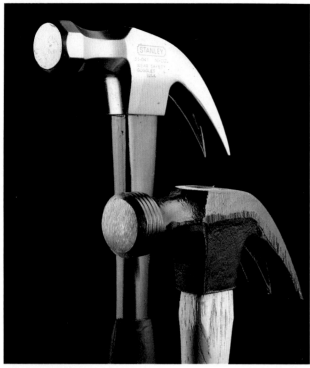

Claw hammer drives and pulls nails. Choose a quality hammer (left) with a 16-ounce head. Look for a smoothly finished, high-carbon steel head. Bargain tool (right) has rougher, painted finish with visible cast marks.

Tack hammer with magnetic head drives small nails or brads that are difficult to hold by hand.

Mallet with rubber or plastic head drives woodworking chisels. Soft mallet face will not damage fine woodworking tools.

Ball peen hammer has heat-treated steel head that resists chipping when driving hardened steel tools or pry bars.

Nail set drives heads of finish and casing nails below wood surface. Choose a nail set with tip that is slightly smaller than nail head.

Nails

The wide variety of nail styles and sizes makes it possible to choose exactly the right fastener for the job. Use either common or box nails for general framing work. Box nails are smaller in diameter, which makes them less likely to split wood. Most common and box nails have a cement or vinyl coating that improves their holding power.

Finish and casing nails have small heads and are driven just below the work surface with a nail set, for projects like nailing wood trim. Casing nails have a slightly larger head than finish nails for better holding power. Galvanized nails have a zinc coating that resists rusting, and are used for outdoor projects.

Other specialty nails are identified by their intended function, like wallboard nails, siding nails, masonry nails, or flooring nails.

Nail lengths are identified by numbers from 4 to 60 followed by the letter "d," which stands for "penny." Some specialty nails are identified by either length or gauge.

Nail Sizes

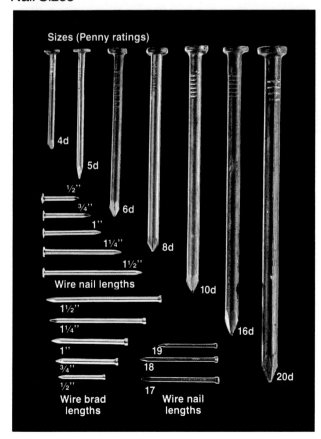

Sizes (Penny ratings)

4d
5d
½"
¾"
6d
1"
1¼"
1½"
8d
Wire nail lengths
10d
1½"
1¼"
16d
1"
19
¾"
18
20d
½"
17
Wire brad lengths
Wire nail lengths

Types of Nails

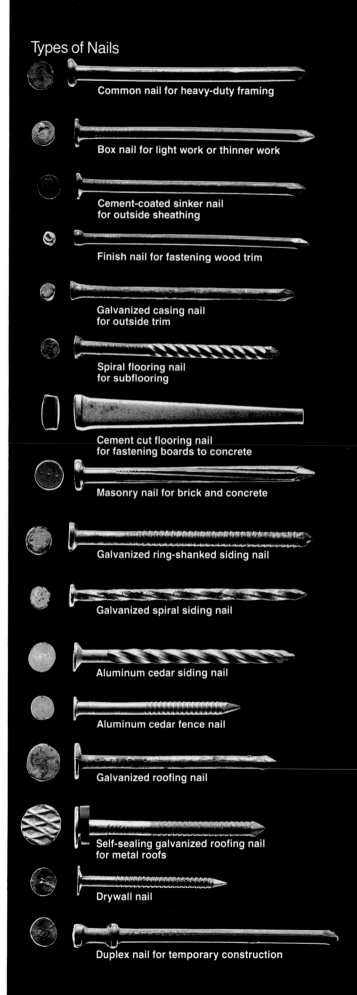

Common nail for heavy-duty framing

Box nail for light work or thinner work

Cement-coated sinker nail for outside sheathing

Finish nail for fastening wood trim

Galvanized casing nail for outside trim

Spiral flooring nail for subflooring

Cement cut flooring nail for fastening boards to concrete

Masonry nail for brick and concrete

Galvanized ring-shanked siding nail

Galvanized spiral siding nail

Aluminum cedar siding nail

Aluminum cedar fence nail

Galvanized roofing nail

Self-sealing galvanized roofing nail for metal roofs

Drywall nail

Duplex nail for temporary construction

Prying Tools

Quality pry bars are made of high-carbon steel, and are available in many sizes. Choose tools forged in a single piece. Tools made from welded parts are not as strong as those that are forged.

Most pry bars have a curved claw at one end for pulling nails and a chisel-shaped tip at the opposite end for other prying jobs. Improve leverage by placing a wood block under the head of pry tools.

Wonderbar® is a slightly flexible tool made of flattened steel. This tool is useful for a variety of prying and wrecking jobs. Both ends can be used for pulling nails.

Prying tools include wrecking bars for heavy demolition work, cat's paws for removing nails, and brad pullers. Wonderbars are made of flattened steel and come in a variety of sizes for light and heavy use.

Wrecking bar, sometimes called a crowbar, is a rigid, heavy-use tool for demolition and heavy prying jobs. Use scrap wood under the bar to protect surfaces.

Cat's paw has a sharpened claw. To extract nails, drive the claw into the wood under the nail head with a hammer.

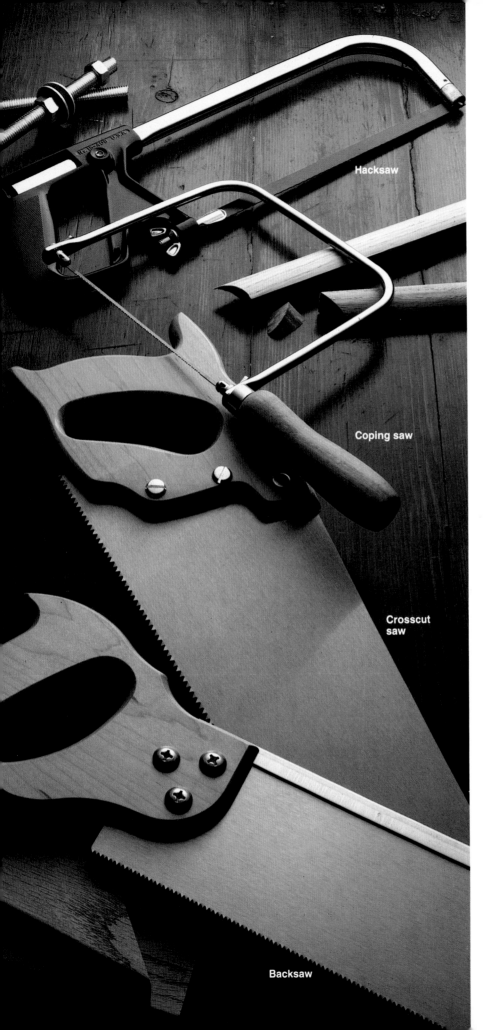

Hacksaw

Coping saw

Crosscut saw

Backsaw

Handsaws

Handsaws can be more practical than portable power saws for small jobs and occasional use.

The crosscut saw is a standard cutting tool designed to cut across the wood grain. A crosscut saw may also be used for occasional "rip" cuts parallel to the wood grain. A crosscut saw with 10 teeth per inch is a good choice for general-purpose cutting.

A backsaw and miter box makes straight cuts. The reinforced spine keeps the backsaw blade from flexing. The miter box locks at any angle for cutting precise miters and bevels.

A coping saw makes curved cuts on materials like wood molding. The coping saw has a very narrow, flexible blade held taut by a C-shaped spring frame. To adjust blade position for scroll cuts, rotate the spigots holding the blade.

Hacksaws are designed to cut metal. Like a coping saw, a hacksaw has a fine, flexible blade that can be replaced when it becomes dull.

Begin handsaw cuts with upward strokes to establish the cut line, then make long, smooth strokes with blade at 45° angle to workpiece. Guide the saw at the beginning of a cut by supporting the edge with the side of your thumb.

Crosscut saw is a standard carpenter's tool. At end of cut, saw slowly and support waste material with a free hand to prevent the wood from splintering.

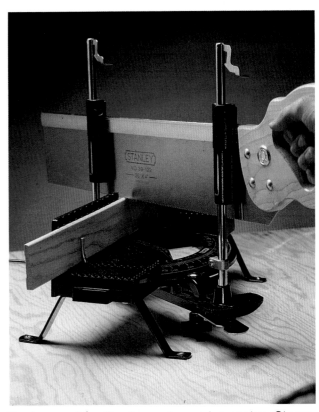

Backsaw with miter box cuts precise angles. Clamp or hold workpiece in miter box. Make certain that miter box is securely fastened to work surface.

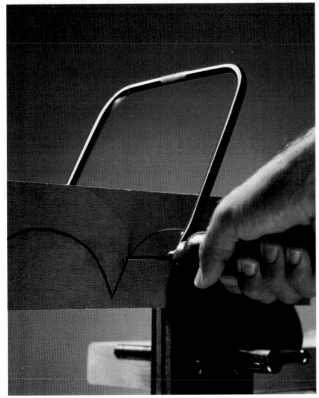

Coping saw has a thin, flexible blade designed to cut curves. It is a necessary tool for cutting and fitting wood moldings.

Hacksaw has a flexible, fine-tooth blade designed to cut metal. Blade must be stretched tightly in frame.

Screwdrivers & Screws

Make sure you have several hand screwdrivers, both phillips and slot types. Quality screwdrivers have hardened-steel blades and wide handles that are easy to grip.

For general use, a cordless power screwdriver saves time and effort. For frequent use, or for large jobs like installing wallboard panels, choose a power screwgun with an adjustable clutch to set screws at different depths.

Screws are categorized according to length, slot style, head shape and gauge. The thickness of the screw body is indicated by the gauge number, from 0 to 24. The larger the gauge number, the larger the screw. Large screws provide extra holding power, while small screws are less likely to split a workpiece. When joining two pieces of wood, choose a screw length so that the entire threaded portion will extend into base piece.

Where appearance is important, use countersink or counterbore bits to drill a recessed hole that will hide the screw head. A countersink bit lets you drive a flat-head screw flush with the wood surface, while a counterbore bit lets you recess the screw head to hide the location with a wood plug.

Common screwdrivers include (from top): stubby model for use in cramped areas, adjustable-clutch screwgun for fastening wallboard, ratchet hand screwdriver with interchangeable bits, cordless power screwdriver with locking spindle, slot screwdriver.

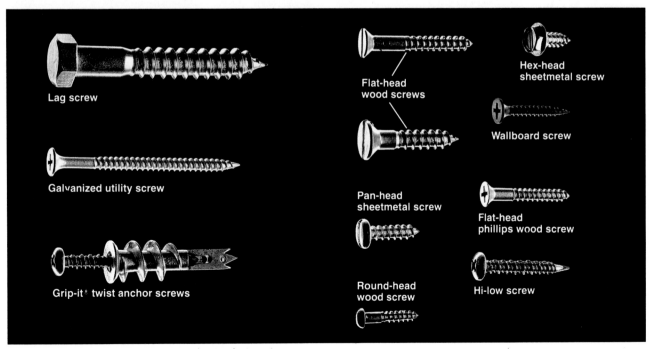

Types of screws: lag screw, galvanized utility screw, Grip-It® twist anchor screws, flat-head wood screws, pan-head sheetmetal screw, oval-head screw, hex-head sheetmetal screw, wallboard screw, flat-head phillips wood screw, hi-low screw.

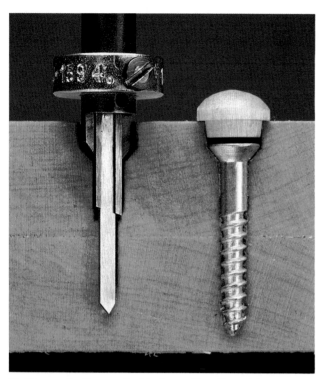

Drill counterbore pilot holes with adjustable counterbore bit. Loosen setscrew and set bit to match length and shape of wood screw. Tighten setscrew and drill until collar reaches surface of workpiece. After driving screw, cover hole with wood plug or putty.

Concrete anchors

Lead anchors

Plastic concrete anchors

Use masonry & wall anchors for attaching to plaster, concrete or brick. Choose an anchor that is equal in length to the thickness of the wall surface.

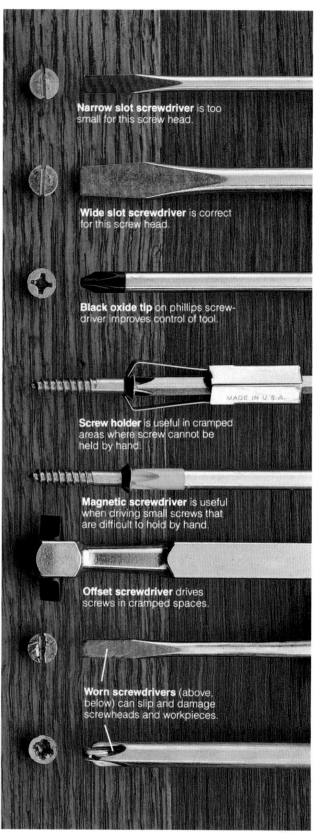

Narrow slot screwdriver is too small for this screw head.

Wide slot screwdriver is correct for this screw head.

Black oxide tip on phillips screwdriver improves control of tool.

Screw holder is useful in cramped areas where screw cannot be held by hand.

MADE IN U.S.A.

Magnetic screwdriver is useful when driving small screws that are difficult to hold by hand.

Offset screwdriver drives screws in cramped spaces.

Worn screwdrivers (above, below) can slip and damage screwheads and workpieces.

Choose proper screwdriver for the job. Screwdriver should fit slot tightly. Common types of screwdrivers include: slot, phillips, phillips with black oxide tip, screw holder, magnetic, and offset screwdrivers.

Drills

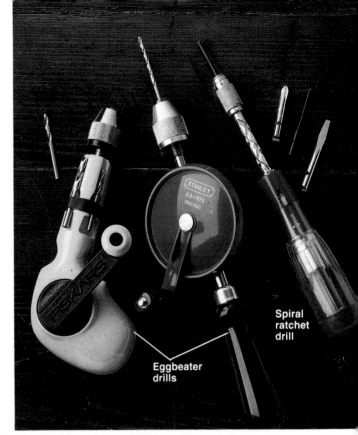

Most drilling jobs can be done easily with a power drill. Power drills are commonly available in ¼-; ⅜- and ½-inch sizes. The number refers to the largest bit shank diameter that fits the drill chuck. A ⅜-inch drill is a good choice because it accepts a wide range of bits and accessories. A variable-speed reversing (VSR) drill will adapt to many uses, like drilling masonry, or driving and removing wallboard screws. A cordless drill offers freedom from extension cords.

When choosing a drill, look for quality features like an extra-long power cord with reinforced cord protector, and a sealed switch that prevents dirt from entering the trigger. A drill that uses top-quality materials may actually be smaller, lighter, and easier to handle than a cheaper drill.

Hand drills include eggbeater and spiral ratchet styles. Hand drills are often used in fine woodworking, or for carpentry jobs where a power drill is not convenient.

Spiral ratchet drill

Eggbeater drills

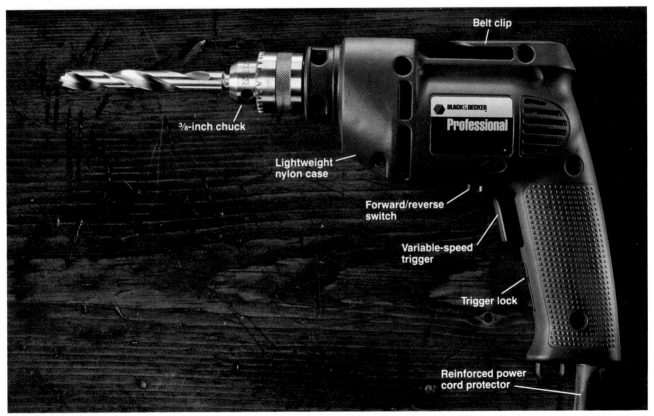

Belt clip

⅜-inch chuck

Lightweight nylon case

Forward/reverse switch

Variable-speed trigger

Trigger lock

Reinforced power cord protector

Power drill features to look for include ⅜-inch chuck size, variable motor speed, reversing feature, trigger lock to set a constant speed, a heavy power cord with reinforced protector, a tough lightweight nylon case, and a molded clip that allows the tool to be hung from a belt or pants pocket.

Drill Bits

Twist bits can be used to bore in both metal and wood. They come in many sizes, ranging from wire gauge to more than ½ inch wide. Some self-piloting bits have a special point for accurate drilling. Most twist bits are made from high-speed or carbon steel. For drilling stainless steel and other hard metals, choose a titanium or cobalt bit.

Spade bits have a long point and flat-edged cutters and are used to cut holes in wood quickly and accurately. Other types of drill bits are available for special applications, like drilling extra-large holes for a lockset, or boring into concrete. Store drill bits so they do not bump against each other, and clean them with linseed oil to prevent rust.

Twist bit can be used in wood or metal. Drill wood at high speeds, metal at low drill speeds.

Self-piloting bit requires no center punch. Special tip reduces splintering in wood, and prevents bit from binding when drilling metal.

Carbide-tipped masonry bit can drill in concrete, cinder block or brickwork. Use low drill speed, and lubricate drill hole with water to prevent overheating.

Glass & tile bit drills smooth holes in smooth, brittle surfaces. Use low drill speed, and wear gloves and eye protection.

Drill saw has twist tip to cut entry hole, and side-cutting rasp teeth for reaming cuts in wood, plastic or light-gauge metals.

Spade bit is used to drill wood. Long tip anchors bit before the cutting edges enter the wood. Begin at low speed, gradually increasing as bit enters wood.

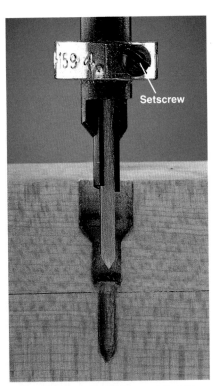

Adjustable counterbore bit drills screw pilot, countersink and counterbore holes with one action. Loosen setscrew to adjust bit to match length and shape of screw.

Setscrew

Plug cutter cuts circular wood plugs used to fill screw counterbore holes.

Mandrel pilot bit

Hole saw with mandrel pilot bit cuts smooth holes in wood, like those used to mount door locksets.

Screwdriver bits, available in many styles, convert a variable-speed drill into a screwgun.

Pilot hole

Extractor bit removes screws with worn or broken heads. Drill a pilot hole into top of screw with twist bit, then use extractor and reverse drill setting to remove screw.

Circular Saw

The power circular saw is ideal for making fast, straight cuts in wood. Special-purpose saw blades make it possible to cut metal, plaster or even concrete with a circular saw. The locking baseplate pivots to adjust blade depth, and rotates for bevel cuts.

Choose a saw with blade size of at least 7¼ inches. A smaller saw may not cut through 2-inch lumber, especially when set at a bevel position. Select a saw with a motor rated at 2 horse-power or more.

Because a circular saw blade cuts as it rotates upward, the top face of the workpiece may splin-ter. To protect the finished side of the workpiece, mark measure-ments on back side of workpiece. Place the good side down, or facing away from the baseplate, when cutting.

Check the cutting angle of circu-lar saw with a T-bevel or square. Make test cuts on scrap wood. If bevel scale is inaccurate, adjust the baseplate to compensate (page opposite).

Use an edge guide for straight, long cuts. Clamp a straightedge on the workpiece. Keep baseplate tight against edge guide and move the saw smoothly.

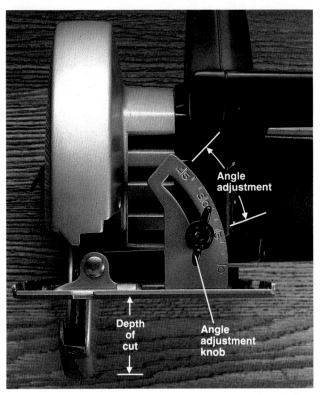

Depth of cut

Angle adjustment

Angle adjustment knob

Set blade angle by loosening the adjustment knob. Set blade depth by loosening adjustment knob at rear of saw. For safety, set the blade so that it projects through bottom of workpiece by no more than the length of one saw tooth. Tighten knobs firmly.

Panel blade for smooth cuts in plywood

Hollow ground planer blade for fine woodworking

Carbide-tipped combination blade

Masonry blade

Metal-cutting blade

Circular saw blades include: carbide-tipped combination blade for general use; panel blade with small teeth which do not chip thin veneer layers in plywood; hollow-ground planer blade with tapered surface that reduces friction, used for fine woodworking; abrasive blades used to cut metal or masonry.

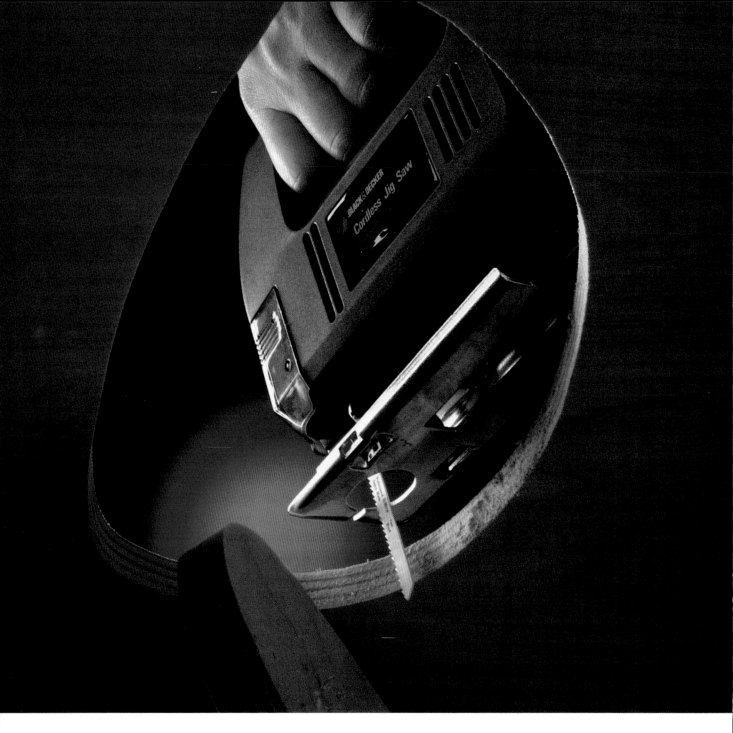

Jig Saw

The jig saw is the best choice for cutting curves. The cutting capacity of a jig saw depends on its power and the length of its blade stroke. Choose a saw rated to cut 2-inch-thick softwood and ¾-inch-thick hardwood stock. Some jig saws have a pivoting baseplate that can be locked to make bevel cuts.

Select a variable-speed jig saw, because different blade styles may require different cutting speeds for best results. In general, use faster blade speeds when cutting with coarse-tooth blades and slower speeds with fine-tooth blades.

A jig saw tends to vibrate because of the up-and-down blade action. A quality jig saw has a heavy-gauge steel baseplate that reduces vibration. To further minimize vibration, hold the saw tightly against the workpiece, and move the saw slowly so the blade does not bend.

Because jig saw blades cut on the upward stroke, the top side of the workpiece may splinter. If the wood has a good side to protect, cut with this surface facing downward.

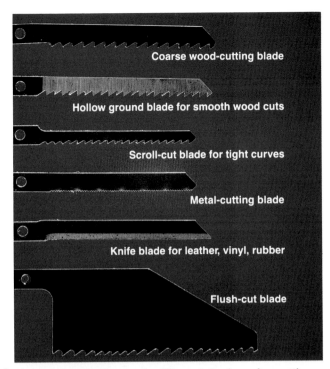

- Coarse wood-cutting blade
- Hollow ground blade for smooth wood cuts
- Scroll-cut blade for tight curves
- Metal-cutting blade
- Knife blade for leather, vinyl, rubber
- Flush-cut blade

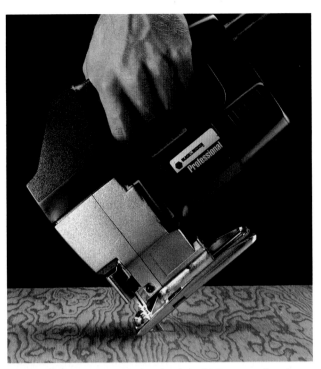

Jig saw blades come in different designs for cutting different materials. Choose a blade that is correct for the job. With fine-tooth blades that have 14 or more teeth per inch, set saw at low blade speed. Coarse blades require faster blade speeds.

Plunge cuts are made by tipping the saw so front edge of the baseplate is held firmly against workpiece. Start saw, and slowly lower it to a horizontal position, letting blade gradually cut through workpiece.

Scrolling knob

Scroll or curved cuts are made with a narrow blade. Move saw slowly to avoid bending the blade. Some jig saws have a scrolling knob that allows the blade to be turned without turning the saw.

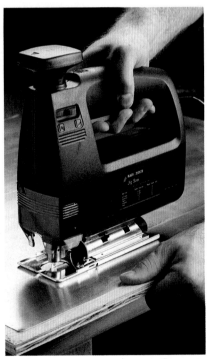

Cut metals with a fine-tooth metal-cutting blade and select a slow blade speed. Support sheet metals with thin plywood to eliminate vibration. Use emery paper or a file to smooth burred edges left by jig saw blade.

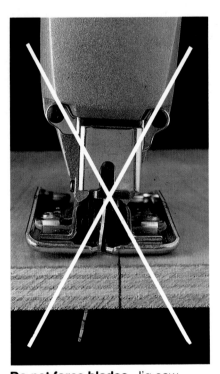

Do not force blades. Jig saw blades are flexible and may break if forced. Move saw slowly when cutting bevels or tough materials like knots in wood.

Check lumber visually before using it. Stored lumber can warp from temperature and humidity changes.

Lumber

Lumber for construction is usually milled from strong softwoods and is categorized by grade, moisture content, and dimension.

Grade: Characteristics such as knots, splits, and slope of the grain affect the strength of the lumber and determine the grade.

Lumber Grading Chart

Grade	Description, uses
SEL STR or select structural 1,2,3	Good appearance, strength and stiffness. 1,2,3 grades indicate knot size
CONST or Construction STAND or Standard	Both grades used for general framing, good strength and serviceability
STUD or Stud	Special designation used in any stud application, including load-bearing walls
UTIL or Utility	Used for economy in blocking and bracing

Moisture content: Lumber is also categorized by moisture content. S-DRY (surfaced dry) is the designation for lumber with a moisture content of 19% or less. S-DRY lumber is the least likely to warp or shrink and is a good choice for framing walls. S-GRN (surfaced green) means the lumber contains a moisture content of 19% or more.

Exterior lumber: Lumber milled from redwood or cedar is naturally resistant to decay and insect attack, and makes a good choice for exterior applications. The most durable part of a tree is the heartwood, so specify heartwood for wood that will be in contact with the ground.

Lumber injected with chemicals under pressure is resistant to decay. Pressure-treated lumber is generally less expensive than redwood or cedar. For outdoor structures like decks, use pressure-treated

28

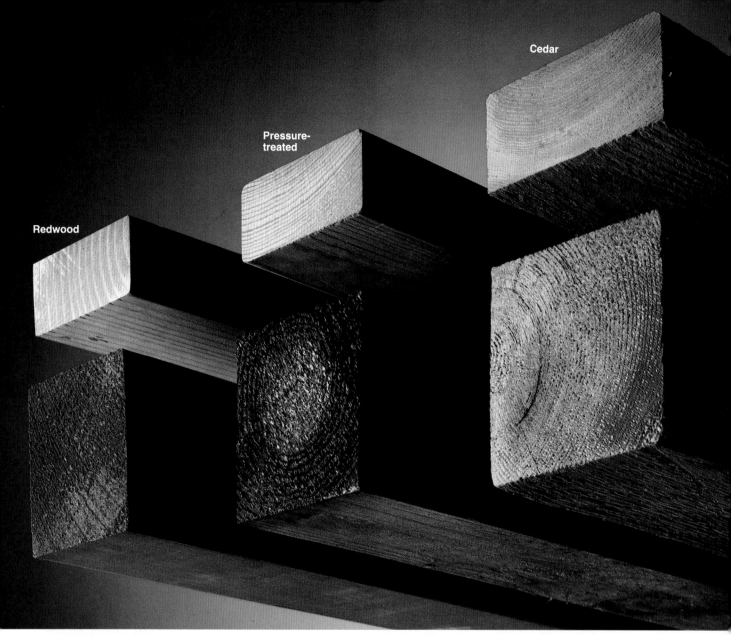

Redwood

Pressure-treated

Cedar

Build longer-lasting outdoor structures by using redwood, pressure-treated lumber or cedar. Redwood and cedar are more attractive, but pressure-treated lumber is less expensive. All are available in common lumber dimensions. Pressure-treated lumber contains toxic chemicals, so wear gloves and a protective particle mask when working with these products.

lumber for posts and joists, and more attractive redwood or cedar for decks and railings.

Dimension: Lumber is sold according to nominal sizes common throughout the industry, such as 2 × 4 and 2 × 6. The actual size of the lumber is smaller than the nominal size.

Nominal vs. Actual Lumber Dimensions

Nominal	Actual
1 × 4	¾" × 3½"
1 × 6	¾" × 5½"
1 × 8	¾" × 7½"
2 × 4	1½" × 3½"
2 × 6	1½" × 5½"
2 × 8	1½" × 7½"

How to Read Lumber Markings

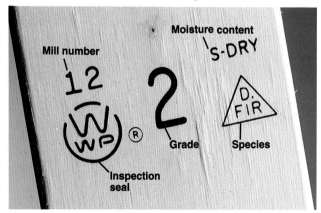

Mill number
Moisture content
S-DRY
12
WWP ®
Inspection seal
2 Grade
D. FIR Species

Check grade stamp on lumber for grade, moisture content and species.

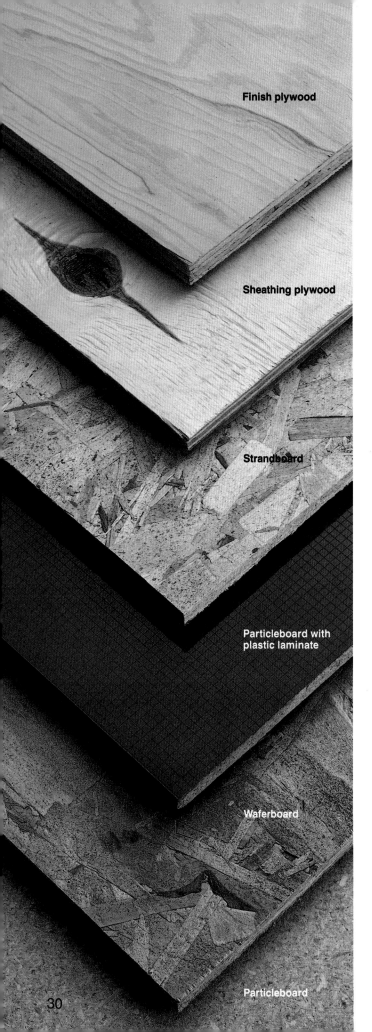

Finish plywood

Sheathing plywood

Strandboard

Particleboard with plastic laminate

Waferboard

Particleboard

Plywood & Sheet Goods

Plywood is a versatile building material made by laminating thin layers or "plies" of wood together and forming them into panels. Plywood is available in thicknesses ranging from 3/16 to 3/4 inch.

Plywood is graded A through D, according to the quality of the wood used on its outer plies. It is also graded for interior or exterior usage. Plywood is classified by group numbers, based on the wood species used for the face and back veneers. Group 1 species are the strongest and stiffest, Group 2 the next strongest.

Finish plywood may have a quality wood veneer on one side and a utility-grade ply on the other side. This will be graded A-C. If it has a quality veneer on *both* sides, the grade will be A-A.

Sheathing plywood is for structural use. It may have large knotholes that make it unsuitable for finish purposes. Sheathing plywood is rated for thickness, and is graded C-D with two rough sides. Sheathing plywood has a waterproof bond. Plywood rated EXPOSURE 1 is for use where some moisture is present. Plywood rated EXTERIOR is used in applications that are permanently exposed to weather. Sheathing plywood also carries a thickness rating and a roof and floor span index, which

How to Read Finish Plywood Markings

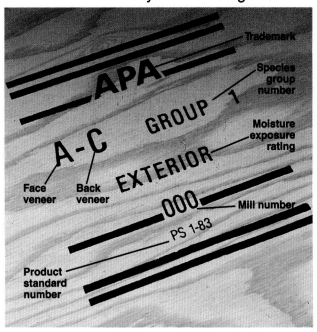

Trademark

Species group number

Moisture exposure rating

Mill number

Face veneer

Back veneer

Product standard number

Finish plywood grading stamp shows the grade of face and back veneers, species group number, and a moisture exposure rating. Mill numbers and product numbers are for manufacturer's use.

appear as two numbers separated by a diagonal slash. The first number, for roofing applications, indicates the widest allowable spacing for rafters. The second number indicates the widest spacing for joists when plywood is used for subflooring.

Strand-, particle-, and waferboards are made from waste chips or inexpensive wood species.

Plastic laminates, like Formica®, are durable, attractive surfaces for countertops and furniture. Particleboard is strong and dimensionally stable, making it an ideal base for plastic laminates.

Plastic foam insulating board is light in weight and provides good insulation for basement walls.

Water-resistant wallboard is made for use in high-moisture areas, like behind ceramic wall tiles.

Wallboard, also known as drywall, Sheetrock®, and plasterboard, comes in panels 4 feet wide by 8, 10, or 12 feet long, and in ⅜-, ½-, and ⅝-inch thicknesses.

Pegboards and hardboards like Masonite® are made from wood fibers and resins bonded together under high pressure.

How to Read Sheathing Plywood Markings

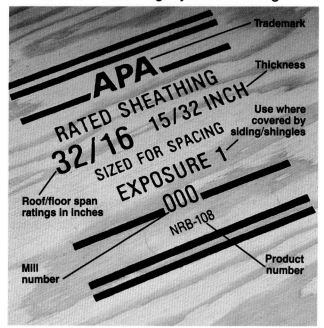

APA
RATED SHEATHING
32/16   15/32 INCH
SIZED FOR SPACING
EXPOSURE 1
000
NRB-108

Trademark
Thickness
Use where covered by siding/shingles
Roof/floor span ratings in inches
Mill number
Product number

Sheathing plywood grading stamp shows thickness, roof or floor span index and exposure rating, in addition to manufacturer's information.

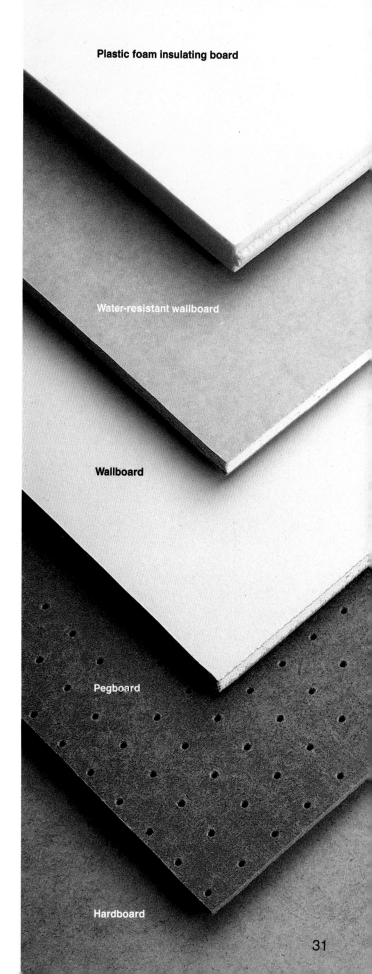

Plastic foam insulating board

Water-resistant wallboard

Wallboard

Pegboard

Hardboard

The Workshop

A dedicated workshop area makes organizing tools and materials easier. It also provides a space where you can work on projects safely and most efficiently.

A good work area is well lighted with 4-foot fluorescent shop lights. The workshop should have an adequate electrical supply, and enough outlets so you will not have to string extension cords everywhere.

Isolate your workshop from living areas, so shop noises and debris will not disturb others. Also, work far away from a forced-air furnace, so that dirt or fumes cannot be sucked into the furnace and circulated through the house.

Store hand tools conveniently by mounting a pegboard hanger above your workbench. Shelves and cabinets are useful for storing power tools and organizing small materials, like screws.

A functional workshop can be as small as a closet or as large as a double-car garage. It can be stocked with a few quality hand tools, or it may contain several stationary power tools costing thousands of dollars. But no matter how varied in appearance, good workshops always reflect careful thought and planning. The tips on the following pages will help you get the most out of your workshop.

When planning a new or remodeled workshop, stock it with common safety equipment. Make sure your workshop has adequate electrical service, with plenty of lighting. Consider how workshop activity affects others in the home. Make sure your shop is well ventilated, and consider soundproofing it for the comfort of others. Finally, learn how to transport building materials efficiently and safely.

Getting a Head

Use a rigid foam head (often used to hold wigs or hats) to store safety equipment. Put the head in a conspicuous place as a reminder to use eye protection, hearing protectors, and other safety gear.

Add-on Outlets

Your workshop should have an ample number of electrical receptacles so tools can be plugged in wherever they are needed. An easy way to add outlets to your workshop is to attach a receptacle strip to the wall above the workbench. One type of receptacle strip plugs into an existing receptacle (below), while others must be wired permanently into a circuit. Some receptacle strips have built-in circuit breakers or fuses to prevent overheating.

Get a Handle on It

Sheets of plywood are heavy and awkward to carry, even with two people. Avoid mishaps and make this job easier by attaching C-clamps to each end of the sheet to use as handles.

Put a Finish to Foot Fatigue

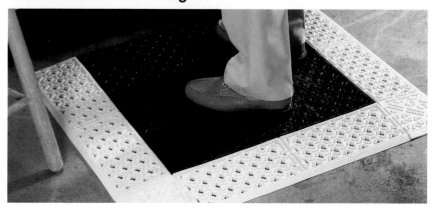

Standing on a concrete workshop floor for long periods of time can tire leg and back muscles. Fatigue also contributes to shop accidents. Reduce muscle strain by laying a resilient rubber anti-fatigue mat, available at industrial tool supply stores, on the floor in front of your work area. Or, use a scrap of old foam-backed carpeting. Wear sturdy, quality work or athletic shoes, and equip your shop with a stool to further reduce fatigue.

Make your shop safer and more convenient by using these lighting and electrical tips. Most of these improvements are easy to make, but if you are uncertain about your own skill level, have a licensed electrician make the changes.

The most common workshop electrical problem is a lack of grounded receptacles. Two-slot receptacles provide no means of grounding, and should be replaced with properly grounded three-slot receptacles. In a basement or garage, the National Electrical Code requires GFCI (ground-fault circuit-interrupter) receptacles. Install additional receptacles or add an electrical circuit if the shop is inadequately wired. A workshop should have at least one duplex receptacle for every 10 ft. of wall space.

In the Spotlight

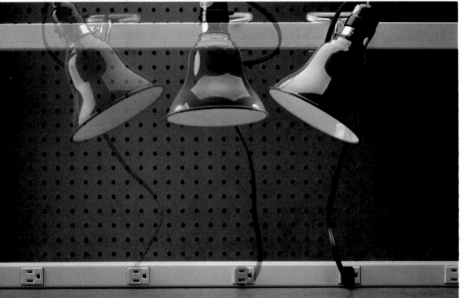

To make your shop lighting scheme more flexible, attach a 2 x 2 furring strip to the wall above the workbench, and mount a clamping arm lamp to the strip. When used with a receptacle strip (page 33), the lamp can be moved along the workbench to spotlight any work area.

Choose the Right Extension Cord (cords under 50 ft.)

Wire gauge	Watt rating	Amp rating	Typical Use
#18	600	5	Power drill, jig saw, hand sander
#16	840	7	Reciprocating saw, belt sander
#14	1440	12	Router, circular saw, miter saw, table saw
#12	1920	16	Radial arm saw, large table saw

Use only heavy-duty extension cords with large power tools. Extension cords are rated by wire gauge, watts, and amps. The smaller the wire gauge, the higher the amp and watt ratings. Make sure that the ratings of the extension cord are equal to or greater than the tool ratings. For extension cords longer than 50 ft., choose the next larger wire gauge.

Pull-apart Prevention

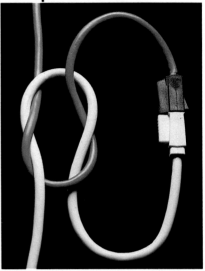

Prevent tool cords from pulling free of electrical extension cords by tying them in a simple knot. Knotting the cords is especially helpful when you are working on a ladder.

Prevent Electrical Shocks

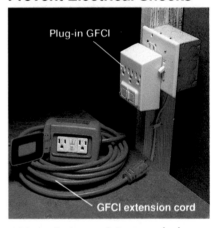

Plug-in GFCI

GFCI extension cord

Although three-slot grounded receptacles provide some protection against shock, for maximum safety it is a good idea to use a GFCI (ground-fault circuit-interrupter) device in conjunction with a grounded receptacle. GFCIs sense small changes in current flow, like those that occur during a short circuit, and shut off power before a shock can occur. Common GFCI devices include plug-in portable GFCIs and GFCI extension cords.

Brighter Lights, Smaller Electrical Bills

Improve visibility in your shop by replacing incandescent lights with fluorescent fixtures. Fluorescent lights provide more light than incandescent lights and are less expensive to operate. Some types of fluorescent light fixtures come with preattached cords for plugging into a receptacle. Other types are permanently wired; you may want to hire an electrician to make permanent installations.

More Power to You

If you are upgrading your electrical service, have an electrician install a subpanel near the shop to control the circuits that serve it. A nearby subpanel is convenient if a circuit breaker trips or a fuse blows. With a subpanel, you can also turn off workshop circuits and lock the subpanel cover to prevent unauthorized tool use.

Dust Caps for Receptacles

Cover unused receptacles by inserting plastic caps into the slots. The caps will keep sawdust and dirt from clogging the receptacle slots—a common cause of short circuits and workshop fires.

Reel Convenience

Prevent extension cord tangles by hanging retractable or reel-type extension cords from overhead hooks. They can be positioned wherever they are needed, and retracted when not in use. Retractable cords are available in lengths ranging from 10 to 30 ft.

Take a Breather

Filter
cartridges

A dual-cartridge respirator protects against toxic vapors, like those from oil-based paints and solvents, and against toxic particles, like asbestos, or sawdust from treated lumber. Correct use of the respirator can prevent lung irritations and disease. Make sure to choose a respirator that is approved by OSHA (Occupational Safety and Health Administration). Use the proper filters in the respirator cartridges, and replace them according to the manufacturer's directions.

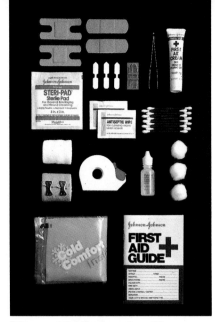

First-aid Kit for the Shop

Keep a well-stocked basic first-aid kit where it can be reached easily. Equip your kit with a variety of bandages, needles and tweezers, antiseptic ointment, cotton swabs, cotton balls, eye drops, a first-aid handbook, a chemical cold pack, elastic bandage, first-aid tape, and sterile gauze. Seek medical help for puncture wounds, cuts, and other serious injuries.

Prevent Workshop Fires

Store flammable materials like solvents and paints in a locked metal cabinet away from sources of heat and flame. Place loose sawdust and wood chips in a covered metal trash can, and empty it frequently. Keep a fire extinguisher in the shop, and maintain it as directed by the manufacturer. Equip the workshop with a smoke detector.

Keep the Lights On

Flying wood chips from a router or power saw can shatter exposed light bulbs and fluorescent tubes. Protect light fixtures by covering them with metal window screening or wire mesh.

A Breath of Fresh Air

Ventilate your workshop so that harmful vapors and fine dust particles are blown out. Many homeowners install permanent exhaust fans, but a simple household fan placed in a window can do the job just as well. For good ventilation, your home workshop should have at least two windows, or one window and a built-in exhaust fan.

Safety Is More Than Skin Deep

Wear rubber gloves when working with solvent-based liquids. Many liquids used in the workshop are powerful skin irritants that can cause burns or blisters. Some of these materials are absorbed through the skin and have been linked to serious health problems. Disposable rubber gloves are available at pharmacies and painting supply stores. Never use gasoline or mineral spirits to clean your skin—try ordinary salad oil instead.

Stay on Your Guard

Never remove the blade guard from a table saw, radial arm saw, or other power tool. A recent survey of professional shop workers revealed that serious accidents rarely occur when blade guards are used correctly.

Key to Safe Tool Use

Prevent children from using power tools by inserting spring-metal key rings through the small holes on the prongs of the plug. Or, use small, key-operated luggage padlocks to safeguard against unauthorized tool use.

The noise generated by some power tools, like circular saws or routers, can reach 115 decibels, enough to cause pain and permanent hearing loss to the listener. Reduce noise hazards by wearing hearing protectors whenever using power tools. Remember, however, that workshop noise is heard easily in other parts of the home. For the comfort and safety of family members, soundproof your shop to muffle the noise.

Noise levels in a home workshop can be controlled by reducing the sound-causing vibrations of power tools. Or, you can soundproof walls and ceilings to prevent noise from being carried to other parts of the home.

Wall constructions are rated for noise by the Sound Transmission Class (STC) system. The higher the STC rating of a wall, the less sound it will transmit. The chart (page opposite) shows different wall constructions, and rates their ability to carry sound.

Deaden Your Doors

Workshop doors with hollow-core construction carry sound well. Deaden sound transmission through a door by attaching acoustical tile to the inside surface. The tiled door surface also can be used as a bulletin board.

Seal Sound Gaps

Air gaps in walls and ceilings can carry sound. To limit the amount of noise (and dust) escaping to other rooms, install door sweeps to seal the gaps underneath workshop doors, install insulating gaskets around electrical outlets, and use fiberglass insulation to plug the holes near water pipes and the spaces between ceiling joists.

Stop Bad Vibes

Motor vibrations carried through metal tool legs to a work surface or floor can increase workshop noise levels. When clamping a tool to a workbench, stop noisy vibrations by placing pads of rubber, pieces of carpet, or rubber furniture cups between the tool legs and bench. Power tool legs that rest directly on the floor also can be padded to reduce vibrations. Also keep tools well oiled to further reduce noise.

Soundproofing Walls & Ceilings (walls shown cut away)	Sound Transmission Class & Comfort Level in Adjacent Room
Typical utility-area stud wall, unfinished on one side.	**STC 28** Power tool noise is loud enough to cause permanent hearing loss with prolonged exposure.
Finish the workshop side of wall with ½" wallboard (A).	**STC 34**
Fill spaces between framing members with fiberglass insulation (B) and cover stud wall with wallboard.	**STC 39**
Add an extra layer of wallboard (C) to the workshop side of the insulated stud wall.	**STC 42**
Attach an extra layer of wallboard to wall, using resilient steel channels (D). Attach channels every 24".	**STC 44**
Attach acoustical tile (E) to the insulated stud wall, using construction adhesive or staples.	**STC 46**
Attach ½" Sound Stop® board (F) and an extra layer of wallboard to walls.	**STC 50** Power tool noise is barely audible.

Transporting building materials from the lumberyard or home center to your home is the first step in any workshop project—and it may be the most difficult. Framing lumber can be tied to a roof carrier rack for transporting, but sheets of plywood, paneling, or wallboard should be delivered by truck. Your lumberyard may deliver your materials for a small additional charge.

If you transport materials on a roof carrier, make sure to tie the load securely. Materials that extend past the rear bumper should be tagged with a red flag to warn drivers behind you. Drive carefully and avoid sudden starts and stops. When using your vehicle to carry heavy loads, like bags of concrete or sand, allow extra braking distance.

All by Yourself

To carry full-size sheets of plywood, paneling, or wallboard by yourself, tie a single length of rope, about 18 ft. long, in a loop. Hook the ends of the loop over the lower corners of the sheet, and grip the middle of the rope in one hand. Use the other hand to balance the sheet.

Cut Problems Down to Size

If you already know the cutting dimensions for plywood, paneling, or other sheet goods, you can make transportation easier by cutting the materials to size while still at the lumberyard or home center. Some lumberyards will cut your materials free of charge. Or, you can bring along a saw and cut the materials yourself.

Up on the Roof

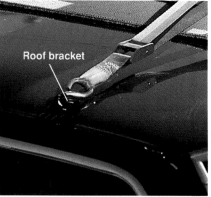

Roof bracket

Tie materials onto the roof of your car using inexpensive, vinyl-coated roof brackets. Hook the brackets over the edge of the roof, then attach nylon packing straps or ropes to the brackets for cinching materials in place. Place carpet scraps under the materials to prevent scratches, and center the load on the car roof.

Most home workshops must fit into an unused utility space—often a cramped area tucked into a basement, garage, or attic. Creating work space and storage areas for tools and materials is a constant challenge. The following pages show you dozens of easy ways to solve common storage problems and organize a new or existing workshop for maximum efficiency. By investing one or two weekends of your time and using inexpensive materials like pegboard, you can turn any cluttered utility area into a functional, enjoyable home workshop.

Pegboard Storage Panel for Stud Walls

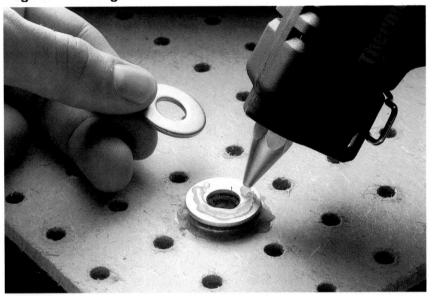

When attaching a pegboard panel to finished walls, hot-glue pairs of washers to the back of the pegboard as spacers, so that pegboard hooks can be inserted. Hang the pegboard panel by anchoring it to every other wall stud, using 2" wallboard screws. Use finish washers (step 3, below) to keep the screw heads from sinking into the pegboard.

Tool Templates

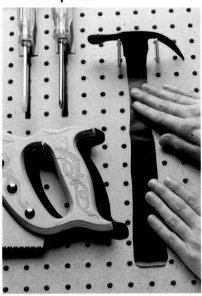

Tool outlines made from contact paper or cardboard can be attached to a pegboard storage panel so tools can be returned to the correct locations after use.

Pegboard Storage Panel for Masonry Walls

Finish washer

1 When attaching pegboard to masonry walls, first measure and cut 1" × 2" furring strips to match the height of the pegboard panel. Apply panel adhesive to one side of each strip. Adhesive will help hold furring strips to the masonry walls.

2 Attach furring strips to wall with 2" masonry nails. For solid support, space the strips no more than 4 ft. apart. For example, a 6-ft.-long pegboard panel requires one furring strip for each end, plus a third strip to support the middle of the panel.

3 Position the pegboard panel against the furring strips. Drive ¾" wallboard screws through the pegboard holes and into the furring strips. Use finish washers to keep the heads of the wallboard screws from sinking into the pegboard.

Use Plastic Bottles for Workshop Storage

Keep clean rags handy for painting and finishing projects by storing them in plastic containers hung from a pegboard storage panel. Rags soaked in mineral spirits or other solvent-based liquids pose a fire hazard. Let dirty rags dry outdoors, then throw them away with household trash.

Storing Saw Accessories

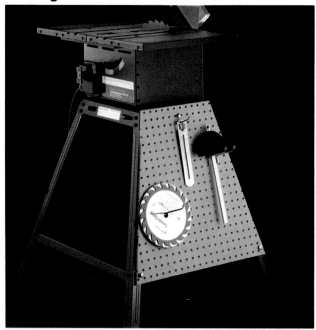

Attach pegboard to the sides of a table saw stand to create storage space for spare saw blades, adjustment wrenches, and other table saw accessories. Attach the pegboard by drilling holes in the legs of the saw stand and mounting the pegboard panel with machine screws and nuts.

Make a Saw Blade Caddy

Use a plywood scrap to make a convenient caddy for storing saw blades and carrying them to a job site. Use a jig saw to cut a carrying handle in the top of the plywood. Drill a 3/8" hole through the center of the plywood, and secure the blades with a 3" carriage bolt, wing nut, and washer. Place cardboard between the blades to protect the teeth from damage.

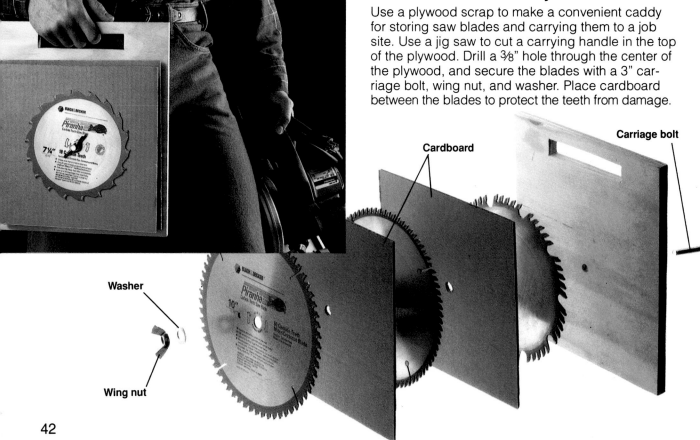

Cardboard

Carriage bolt

Washer

Wing nut

Bench Buddy

Create more storage space by attaching pieces of pegboard to the sides of the workbench with wallboard screws and finish washers.

Hide-away Hangers

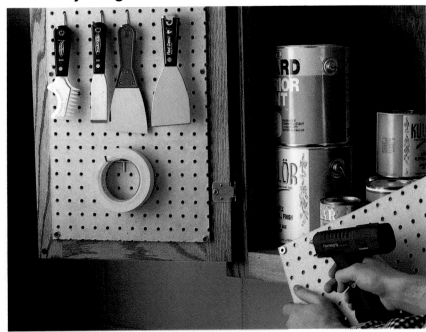

The inside surface of cabinet doors is an overlooked storage area. To make use of this space, attach small pegboard panels with ½" wallboard screws. Glue pairs of metal washers on the back of the pegboard as spacers to provide room for pegboard hooks to be inserted (page 41).

Bit by Bit

Metal drill and router bits have finely honed cutting edges which can be ruined if the bits bump against each other inside a toolbox or workbench drawer. To protect tool bits from damage, make a storage block by boring holes in a scrap piece of lumber. Attach screw eyes to the top of the block so it can be stored on pegboard hooks and taken down when a bit is needed.

Up Against the Wall

Add storage space in an unfinished utility area by covering the studs with panels of pegboard. These panels are ideal for storing wallboard framing squares, levels, garden tools, and other large items.

43

Stick 'em Up

Attach magnetic strips to the front of a workbench to store small metal tools, hardware items, tool wrenches, or drill chuck keys. Magnetic strips also can be attached to a metal table saw stand or other stationary tool. You can purchase these powerful magnetic strips at hardware or cutlery stores.

Keep Your Cap On

The caps that come with glues, caulks, and other shop products are easy to lose. Replace lost caps with screw-on electrical wire nuts. Wire nuts, available in many sizes, can be purchased at any hardware store.

Glued Clues

Most workshops have dozens of small containers holding screws, nails, bolts, and other hardware. To locate items quickly and easily, use a hot glue gun to stick a sample of the contents on the outside of each bag or box.

Sanding Belt Storage

Sanding belts stored in a drawer or toolbox can get creased or flattened and lose their effectiveness. To avoid this, hang sanding belts from old paint-roller covers or pieces of PVC plumbing pipe attached to pegboard hooks.

Fallout Protection

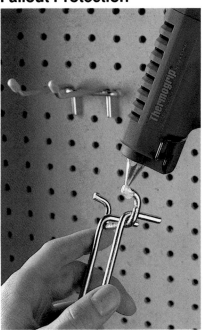

Pegboard hooks frequently fall out when an item is removed. End this aggravating problem by gluing the hooks to the pegboard with a hot glue gun. If you need to reposition the pegboard hooks, heat them for a few seconds with a heat gun until the glue softens.

Beat the Tangle Tussle

Extension cords and power tool cords often become knotted and tangled. To keep a cord neatly coiled, cut off the ends of a clean plastic motor oil bottle, and slip it over the coiled electrical cord. Or secure cords with the ties from plastic garbage bags.

Out of Sight, Easy to Find

Make use of storage space underneath a stairway. Build a simple plywood shelf and attach it to the stairway stringers to store tool manuals, small cans, and bottles. Attach nails and hooks to risers for storing rolls of tape, paint brushes, putty knives, and other small tools.

Clever Cord Carrier

Keep extension cords tangle-free by storing them in 5-gallon plastic buckets. Cut a hole in the side of the bucket near the bottom. Thread the pronged extension cord plug through the hole from the inside, then coil the cord into the bucket. The extension cord will remain tangle-free when pulled from the bucket. You can also use the bucket to carry tools to a work site.

Bit Bed

Protect and organize expensive router bits by lining a workbench drawer with rigid foam or foam rubber. Cut out recesses in the foam so the finely honed cutting edges do not bump against other objects.

Pipe Dream

Organize a collection of pipe clamps and bar clamps by storing them on a 2 × 4 attached to wall studs. Anchor the 2 × 4 to the studs with 3" wallboard screws or lag screws.

Waste-not Storage Boxes

Use leftover pieces of plywood or 1" lumber to build sturdy storage boxes for heavy hardware. Assemble the boxes with 1¼" wallboard screws. Organize the storage boxes on utility shelves for easy access. If you wish, attach metal handles to the boxes. Wooden drawers from a discarded desk or dresser also make good storage boxes.

Hang 'em High

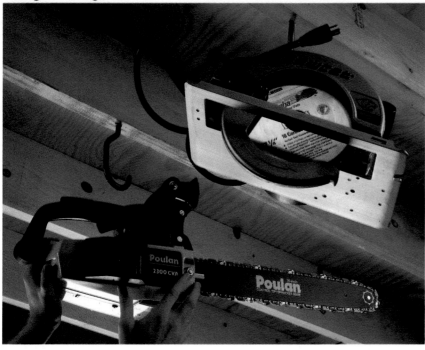

Use large, rubber-coated lag hooks to store power tools off the floor and away from dirt and moisture. Anchor the lag hooks securely to ceiling joists or cross blocking.

How to Coil Long Extension Cords

1 Hold the end of the extension cord in one hand. Use the other hand to loop the extension cord back and forth in a figure-eight pattern until it is completely coiled.

2 Take one of the cord loops and wrap it twice around one end of the coil.

3 Insert the loop though the center of the coil, and pull it tight. Store the cord by hanging it from this loop.

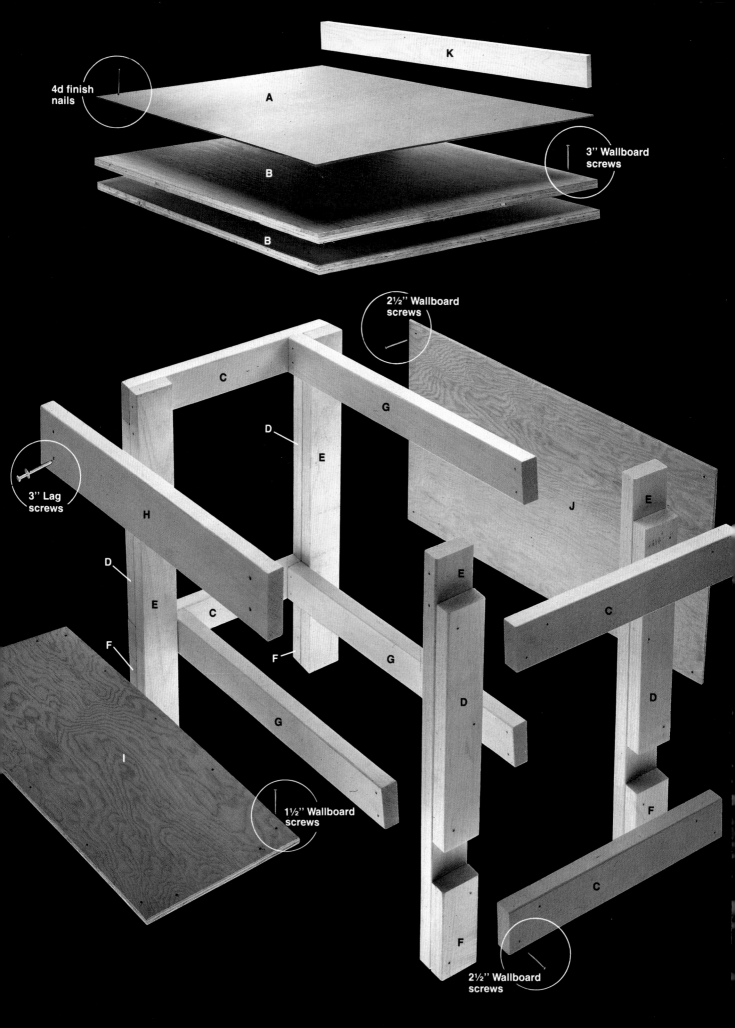

4d finish nails

3" Wallboard screws

2½" Wallboard screws

3" Lag screws

1½" Wallboard screws

2½" Wallboard screws

A

K

B

B

C

D

E

G

D

H

E

F

C

F

G

J

E

E

C

D

G

D

F

I

G

F

C

Building a Workbench

This workbench has heavy-duty legs to support big loads, and a sturdy double-layer top to withstand pounding. Cover the top with a hardboard surface that can be removed when it becomes damaged. Build a shelf below the work surface for storing power tools. If desired, mount an all-purpose vise bolted to the front or top of the workbench.

Before You Start:
Tools & Materials: circular saw, carpenter's square, wallboard screws (1½-, 2½-, and 3-inch), screwgun or cordless screwdriver, drill and bits, lag screws (1½- and 3-inch), ratchet or adjustable wrench, 4d finish nails, nail set.

Tip: A workbench can be equipped with useful accessories, like pegboard screwed to the bench ends for storing saw blades and small tools, or woodworking vises.

Lumber List: six 8-foot 2 × 4s, one 5-foot 2 × 6, one 4 × 8-foot sheet of ¾" plywood, one 4 × 8-foot sheet of ½" plywood, one 4 × 8-foot sheet of ⅛" hardboard. Use a framing square to mark pieces, and cut with circular saw to dimensions indicated below.

KEY	Pcs	SIZE AND DESCRIPTION
A	1	⅛-inch hardboard top, 24" × 60"
B	2	¾-inch plywood top, 24" × 60"
C	4	2 × 4 crosspieces, ends, 21"
D	4	2 × 4 legs, 19¾"
E	4	2 × 4 legs, 34½"
F	4	2 × 4 legs, 7¾"
G	3	2 × 4 braces, 54"
H	1	2 × 6 front (top) brace, 57"
I	1	½-inch plywood shelf, 14" × 57"
J	1	½-inch plywood shelf back, 19¼" × 57"
K	1	1 × 4 backstop, 57"

How to Build a Workbench

1 For each end, cut two each of pieces C, D, E, and F. Assemble with 2½-inch wallboard screws.

2 Attach both 2 × 4 rear braces (G, G) inside back legs of assembled ends. Use 2½-inch wallboard screws.

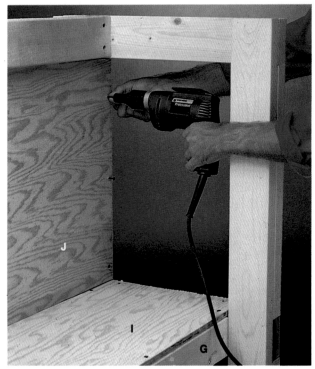

3 Attach 2 × 4 front lower brace (G) inside front legs of assembled ends. Secure bottom shelf (I) and workbench back (J) with 2½-inch wallboard screws to assembled 2 × 4 frame.

4 Drill pilot holes and join 2 × 6 front upper brace (H) outside front legs with 3-inch lag screws.

5 Center bottom layer of ¾-inch plywood work surface (B) on top of frame. Align with back edge, and hold in place with 4d nails.

6 Align bottom and top layers of plywood work surface (B, B). Drive 3-inch wallboard screws through both layers into bench frame.

7 Nail hardboard work surface covering (A) to plywood substrate (B, B) with 4d finish nails. Set nails below surface.

How to Mount a Tabletop Bench Vise

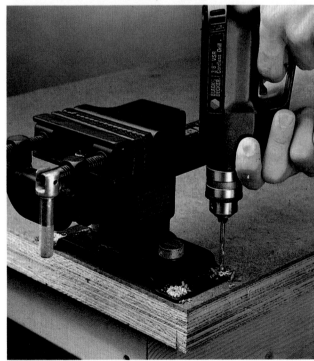

1 Position vise at end of bench. On bench top, mark holes in vise base. Bore ¼-inch holes into bench top to secure vise.

2 Attach vise with 1½-inch lag screws. Attach backstop (K) to back of bench top, with 2½-inch wallboard screws.

Sawhorses

Sawhorses are used to support work materials for marking and cutting. They can also form the base for sturdy temporary scaffolding to use while painting or installing wallboard. For scaffolding, place good-quality 2 × 10s or 2 × 12s across two heavy-duty sawhorses. Small break-down sawhorses are a good choice if storage space is limited.

Before You Start:
Tools & Materials: four 8-foot 2 × 4s, 2½-inch wallboard screws, circular saw, framing square, screwgun or cordless screwdriver.

Lumber Cutting List

KEY	Pcs	SIZE AND DESCRIPTION
A	2	Vertical braces, 2 × 4, 15½"
B	2	Top rails, 2 × 4, 48"
C	1	Bottom brace, 2 × 4, 48"
D	2	Horizontal braces, 2 × 4, 11¼"
E	4	Legs, 2 × 4, 26"

Easy-storing Sawhorses

Fold metal sawhorses and hang them on the workshop wall when they are not in use.

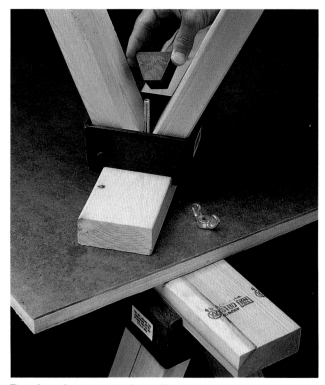

Buy brackets made from fiberglass or metal, and cut a 48-inch top rail and four 26-inch legs from 2 × 4s. Take sawhorses apart for storage.

How to Build a Heavy-duty Sawhorse

1 Heavy-duty sawhorse has wide top for supporting large loads. Cut vertical braces (A), top rails (B), and bottom brace (C) to lengths specified in Lumber Cutting List (page opposite).

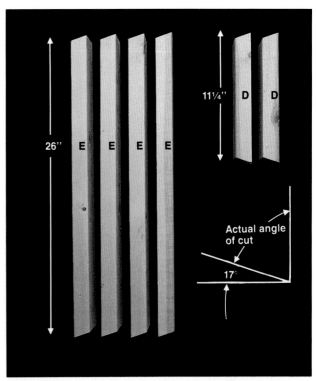

2 Set circular saw to 17° bevel angle. (Bevel cuts will match angle shown above.) Cut ends of horizontal braces (D) with opposing angles. Cut ends of legs (E) with parallel angles.

3 Attach top rails (B) to vertical braces (A), as shown, using 2½-inch wallboard screws.

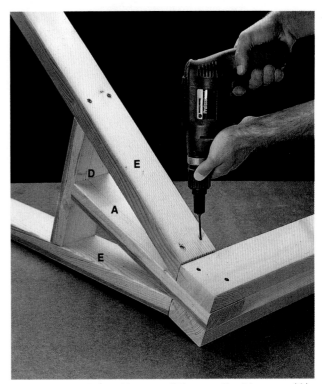

4 Attach horizontal braces (D) to vertical braces (A), using 2½-inch wallboard screws. Attach legs (E). To complete sawhorse, attach bottom brace (C) to horizontal braces (D).

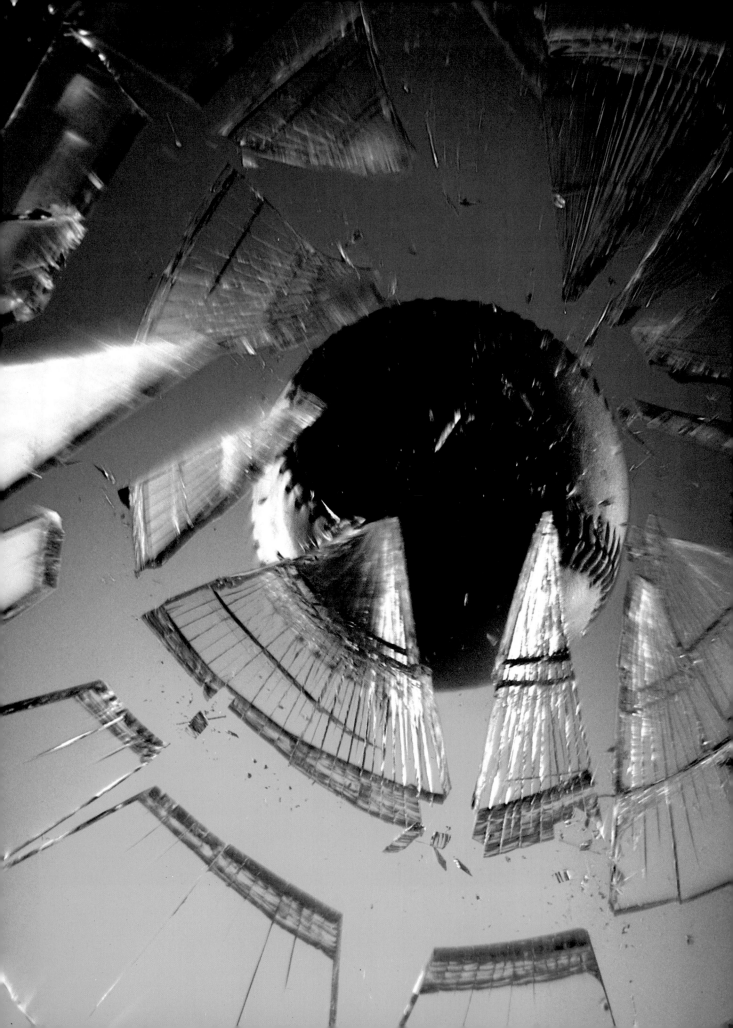

Windows & Doors

Repairing Windows & Doors

Eighty percent of all problems with window or door hardware are caused by lack of lubrication. Clean the moving parts of doors with a combination solvent/lubricant spray. Clean the tracks on double-hung and aluminum windows with an old toothbrush and a dust cloth or hand vacuum. Lubricate window tracks with a greaseless lubricant containing silicone or graphite.

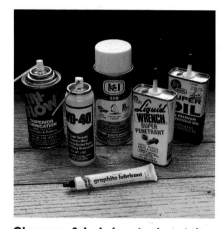

Cleaners & Lubricants, from left: spray solvent/lubricant, penetrating spray, silicone spray, penetrating oils, powdered graphite (front center).

Tools for Windows & Doors

Cleaning & Lubricating Tips

Clean the tracks on sliding windows and doors with a hand vacuum and a toothbrush. Dirt buildup is common on storm window tracks.

Clean weatherstrips by spraying with cleaner and wiping away dirt. Use paint solvent to remove paint that may bind windows. Apply a small amount of lubricant to prevent sticking.

Lubricate locksets and hinges once each year by taking them apart and spraying with solvent/lubricant. Lubricate new locksets before installing them.

How to Clean & Lubricate Sliding Doors

1 Clean the tracks with a toothbrush and damp cloth or hand vacuum.

2 Spray a solvent/lubricant on all the rollers. Replace any bent or worn parts.

Mounting screw

3 Check gap along bottom edge of door to make sure it is even. To adjust the gap, rotate the mounting screw to raise or lower the door edge.

How to Lubricate & Adjust Bifold Doors

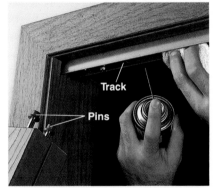

Track

Pins

1 Open or remove the doors and wipe the tracks with a clean rag. Spray the track and rollers or pins with greaseless lubricant.

Pivot block

2 Check closed doors for alignment within the door frame. If gap between closed doors is not even, adjust the top pivot blocks with a screwdriver or wrench.

Pivot block

Adjustable pivot blocks are also found at the bottom of some door models. Adjust pivot block until gap between door and frame is even.

How to Lubricate Garage Doors

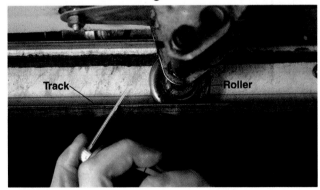

Track

Roller

1 Clean the rollers and door tracks with a cloth, then spray with lubricant. Tighten any loose screws, bolts or nuts. **Do not** tamper with the steel springs: they are under high tension, and should be adjusted by a professional.

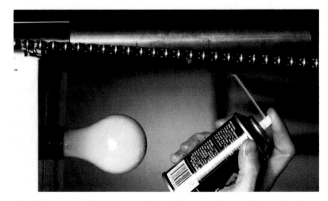

2 Clean and lubricate the drive chain and track of an automatic opener. Check manufacturer's instructions for additional maintenance directions.

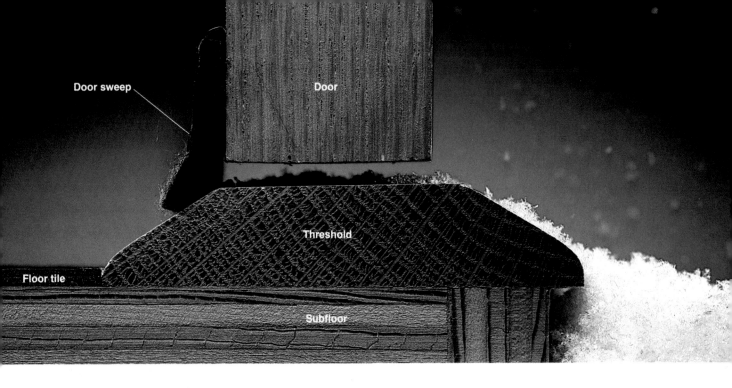

Installing New Weatherstripping

Weatherstripping seals cracks between jointed or moving materials — between the window and frame, or between the door and its frame or threshold. Weatherstripping keeps dirt, insects and cold air outside your house, and keeps conditioned air (heated or cooled) inside the home. It also silences rattling doors or windows.

New weatherstripping is always a wise investment. The money you save on fuel costs in a single heating season far exceeds the purchase price of the weatherstripping.

Weatherstripping is made of a variety of materials: foam plastic, vinyl or plastic. Most types of weatherstripping are sold in kits that contain all the nails or screws needed for installation.

Before You Start:

Tools & Materials: new weatherstripping, hammer, screwdriver, tin snips, hacksaw, drill, pry bar.

Types of Weatherstripping

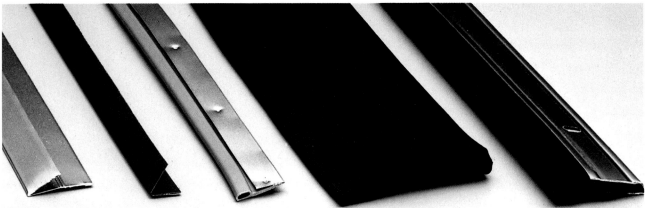

Spring metal provides a seal between a door and frame.

Adhesive vinyl v-stripping can be used on windows or doors.

Metal & vinyl may contain felt and attaches to window frame.

Garage door weatherstrip seals out water, dirt and insects.

Door sweeps seal gap between a door and threshold.

How to Install a Door Sweep

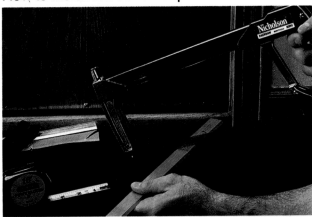

1 Measure the width of the door. Cut a new sweep with a hacksaw so that the sweep is ⅛ inch narrower than width of the door.

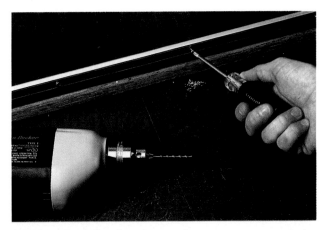

2 Drill pilot holes for screws, then screw sweep to inside of door so that felt or vinyl blocks gap under door. Slotted screw holes allow adjustment.

How to Install Garage Door Weatherstrip

1 Remove the cracked or brittle weatherstrip by prying out old nails.

2 Cut new weatherstrip to fit door. Nail strip to bottom of door with noncorroding galvanized nails.

How to Install Spring-metal Door Stripping

1 Cut metal strips to fit the top and both sides of the door frame (jamb). Open V of strip faces outdoors.

2 Nail strips in place with slight gap between the metal and door stop. Spring metal compresses to seal air leaks when door closes.

3 Pry metal outward slightly with screwdriver to assure tight seal. Do this before each heating season, because strip gradually loses its spring.

How to Install Adhesive Vinyl V-stripping

Side sash

Bottom sash

Channels

1 Clean the window sashes and channels with a dry cloth. Remove any worn weatherstripping.

2 Cut vinyl v-strips for the window channels. Strips should measure 2 inches longer than window sash. Crease each strip into a V shape.

Crack

Channel

3 Open lower window fully. Tuck top end of v-strips into cracks between window and channel, with open V facing outdoors. Peel off liner, beginning at bottom, and press v-strip in place.

4 Cut strip to fit bottom sash. Peel liner and press v-strip onto bottom sash.

5 Cut v-strip to fit the lock rail of the top window. Crease strip, then peel liner.

6 Press v-strip into place. Open V of strip should face down. On newer double-hung windows, the bottom window can be removed to install v-strips.

How to Install Metal & Vinyl Stripping

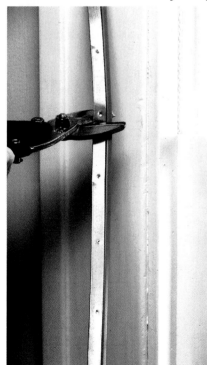

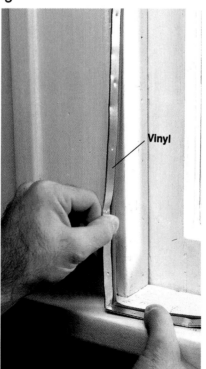

1 Cut the strip long enough so that one piece will seal entire opening.

2 Bend strip sharply to fit corners. Press strip against window sash so that vinyl compresses slightly.

3 Nail weatherstrip around opening. At corners, nail close to corner to assure tight seal.

61

Repairing Loose or Sticking Windows

Windows stick because the channels or guides need cleaning and lubricating, or because they have been painted shut.

Loose windows that refuse to stay open may have broken sash cords or chains.

Newer double-hung windows are balanced by springs, and have adjustment screws to control window movement.

Before You Start:

Tools & Materials: paint zipper or utility knife, hammer, screwdriver, small pry bar, sash cord.

Tips for Freeing a Sticking Window

Paint zipper

Stop

Sash

Cut paint film, if window is painted shut. Insert a paint zipper or utility knife into crack between window stop and sash.

Sash

Place block of scrap wood along window sash. Tap lightly with a hammer to free window.

How to Adjust Spring-loaded Windows

Track insert

Adjust screw found on track insert. Turn screw until window is properly balanced.

How to Replace Broken Sash Cords

1 Cut any paint seal between the window frame and stops using a utility knife or paint zipper. Pry stops away from frame with small pry bar, or remove molding screws.

2 Bend stops in a slight curve from center of frame to remove them. Remove any metal weatherstripping by pulling nails holding strips in channel.

3 Slide out the lower window. Pull knotted or nailed cords from holes in side window sashes.

4 Pry out or unscrew cover of weight pocket found in lower end of window channel. Reach inside pocket and remove the weight. Remove old sash cord from weight.

5 Tie piece of string to small nail. Tie other end of string to new sash cord. Run nail over the pulley wheel and let it drop into weight pocket. Retrieve nail and string through open pocket.

6 Pull on string to run new sash cord over pulley wheel and through weight pocket. Make sure new cord runs smoothly over pulley wheel.

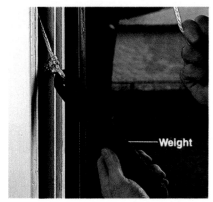

7 Attach end of new sash cord to the weight using a tight double knot. Return the weight to the open pocket and pull on sash cord to raise weight up against pulley.

8 Rest bottom window on sill. Hold sash cord firmly against side of window, and cut enough cord to measure 3 inches past hole in side window sash.

9 Knot sash cord and wedge knot into hole in window sash. Replace the pocket cover. Slide window and weatherstripping back into frame. Nail weatherstripping and replace stops.

Replacing Glass

To replace broken glass, first remove the glazing putty and glazing points, then carefully remove the glass. Take the exact measurements of the opening to the hardware store. Remember that the replacement glass should measure ¼ inch less in each direction than the actual opening. This provides a ⅛-inch expansion space on each edge of the installed glass.

Seal the bare wood before installing new glass to prevent wood rot and to assure the glazing does not dry out prematurely. New types of glazing are applied by a caulk gun and are easier to work with than old-style glazing putty.

Before You Start:

Tools & Materials: heat gun, gloves, eye protection, putty knife, sandpaper, wood sealer, sash brush, replacement glass, glazing points, tube-style glazing compound, caulk gun.

Tip: To avoid injury, wear gloves and eye protection when removing broken glass from sashes, or handling new glass.

How to Install New Glass

1 Remove spring-loaded double-hung windows by pushing against flexible vinyl channels to release channel pins. Older double-hung windows can be repaired while window remains in frame.

2 With traditional glazing, soften old putty with heat gun or torch, being careful not to scorch wood. Scrape away soft putty with a putty knife. On newer windows, pry out the vinyl glazing strips.

3 Remove the broken glass and metal glazing points from the frame, then sand the L-shaped grooves to clean away old paint and putty. Coat bare wood with sealer and let dry.

4 Apply a thin layer of glazing compound in the primed grooves. Press glass lightly to bed it. Press in new glazing points every 10 inches with tip of putty knife.

5 Apply glazing compound. Move the tube tip along the edge of the glass while steadily squeezing the trigger. Smooth the glazing with wet finger or cloth.

6 Latex glazing can be painted the same day. Overlap the paint onto the glass by 1/16 inch to improve its weather seal.

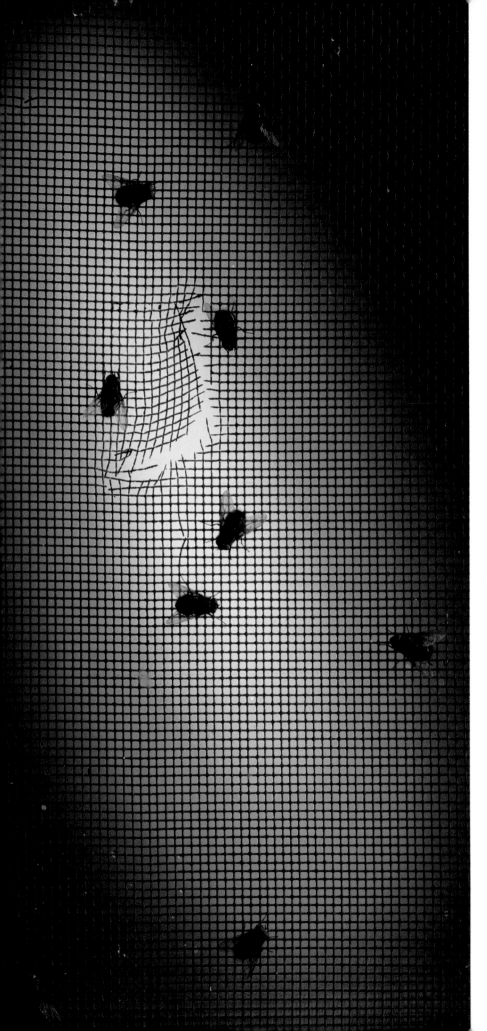

Replacing Screens

Replace the old metal screening with new fiberglass sunscreen. This blocks sunlight to keep the house cooler and prevent fabric fading. Modern screens are corrosion-resistant and maintenance-free.

Before You Start:

Tools & Materials for Wooden Frames: small chisel or screwdriver, utility knife, screen fabric, stapler or thumbtacks, wire brads, hammer.

Tools & Materials for Aluminum Frames: screwdriver, screen fabric, vinyl spline, spline roller, utility knife.

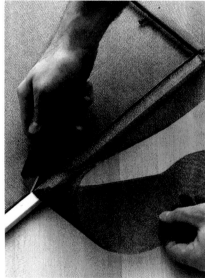

Screen repair tip: For easy handling, cut screen fabric larger than opening, then trim after screen molding or spline is reinstalled.

How to Replace a Screen in a Wooden Frame

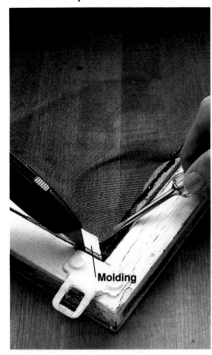

1 Pry up screen molding with a small chisel or screwdriver. If molding is sealed with paint, use a utility knife to cut the paint film and free the molding.

2 Stretch the new screen fabric tightly across the frame and hold it in place with staples or thumbtacks.

3 Nail the screen molding back in place with wire brads. Cut away excess screen fabric with a utility knife (page opposite).

How to Replace a Screen in an Aluminum Frame

1 Pry vinyl spline from grooves around edge of frame with a screwdriver. Retain the old spline, if it is still flexible, or replace with new spline.

2 Stretch the new screen fabric tightly over the frame so that it overlaps the retaining grooves.

3 Use a spline roller to press spline and screen into grooves. Cut away excess screen fabric with a utility knife (page opposite).

Repairing a Lockset

How to Clean & Lubricate Locksets

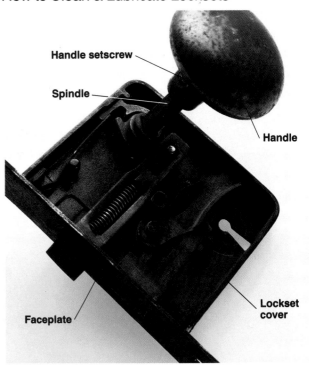

Handle setscrew

Spindle

Handle

Faceplate

Lockset cover

Most lockset problems are solved by cleaning away dirt buildup, then lubricating the inner parts with an all-purpose solvent/lubricant.

When a door will not latch even though the lockset is working smoothly, look for problems with the wood, hinges, strike plate or frame (pages 70-73).

Before You Start:

Tools & Materials: screwdriver, spray solvent/lubricant.

Tip: If the handle on an older passage lock falls off the spindle, rotate handle to different position on spindle, and retighten setscrew.

Older passage lockset. Loosen handle setscrew and remove handles and attached spindle. Loosen faceplate screws and pry lockset from door. Remove lockset cover or faceplate. Spray solvent/lubricant on all parts. Wipe away the excess lubricant and reassemble lockset.

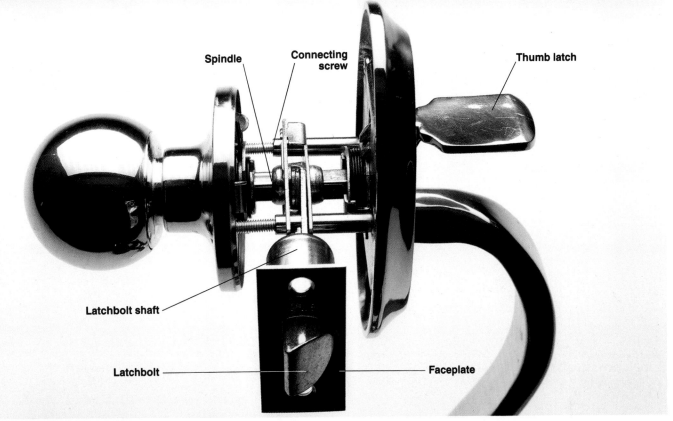

Spindle

Connecting screw

Thumb latch

Latchbolt shaft

Latchbolt

Faceplate

Locksets operate by extending a **latchbolt** through a **faceplate** into a strike plate set into the doorframe. The latchbolt is moved back and forth by a **spindle** or connecting rod operated by a **thumb latch, handle,** or a keyed cylinder.

If a doorknob or key binds when turned, the problem usually lies in the **spindle and latchbolt mechanism.** Cleaning and lubricating the moving parts will correct most problems.

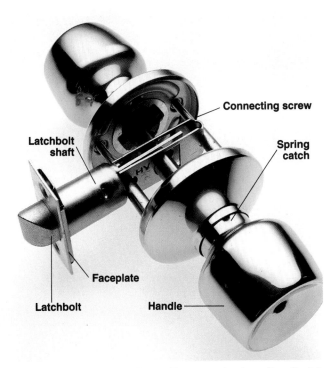

Connecting screw

Spring catch

Latchbolt shaft

Faceplate

Latchbolt

Handle

Modern passage lockset. Remove the handles (held by connecting screws or spring catch). Loosen the retaining screws to remove the faceplate and latchbolt shaft. Spray solvent/lubricant on all parts. Wipe away the excess lubricant and reassemble lockset.

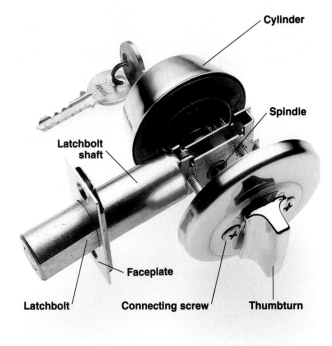

Cylinder

Spindle

Latchbolt shaft

Faceplate

Latchbolt

Connecting screw

Thumbturn

Security locks. Loosen connecting screws to remove inside and outside cylinders. Loosen retaining screws to remove faceplate and latchbolt shaft. Spray solvent/lubricant on all parts. Wipe away the excess lubricant and reassemble lockset.

Sticking latchbolt is caused by dirt and lack of lubrication. Clean and lubricate lockset (pages 69-70). Make sure connecting screws on lockset are not too tight. An overly tightened screw will cause latchbolt to bind.

Common Causes of Door Latch Problems

Misalignment with strike plate prevents latchbolt from extending into strike plate opening. First, check for loose hinges (page 73). To align strike plate and latchbolt, see opposite page.

Door Latch Repairs

Latching problems occur when the **latchbolt** binds within the **faceplate**, or when the latchbolt does not slide smoothly into the strike plate opening.

First, make sure the lockset is clean and lubricated (page 69). If latching problems continue, align the latchbolt and strike plate.

Before You Start:

Tools & Materials: metal file, cardboard shims, weights, wood sealer.

Tip: If a latchbolt and strike plate are badly out of alignment, check for problems with the hinges (pages 72-73).

Warped door caused by humidity or water penetration can cause latching problems. Check for warping with a straightedge. To straighten a warped door, see opposite page.

How to Align Latchbolt & Strike Plate

1 Fix any loose hinges (page 73) and test door. Fix minor alignment problems by filing the strike plate until the latchbolt fits.

2 Check the door for square fit. If the door is badly tilted, then remove the door (page 72) and shim the top or bottom hinge (right).

3 Raise position of latchbolt by inserting thin cardboard shim behind bottom hinge. To lower latchbolt, shim behind top hinge.

How to Straighten a Warped Door

1 Remove door (page 72). Support both ends of warped door on sawhorses. Place heavy weights on bowed center. Leave door weighted for several days until bow is straightened. Check door with straightedge (page opposite).

2 Apply clear sealer to the ends and edges of door to prevent moisture from entering wood in the future. Rehang the door.

Hinge pin

Freeing a Sticking Door

Doors stick when the hinges sag, or when the wood of the door or door frame swells or shifts.

Make sure the door hinge screws are tight. If a door continues to stick after you tighten the hinges, wait for dry weather to sand or plane the door. If the sticking problem occurs only during unusually wet weather, wait for a dry period, then seal the door edges. This should solve occasional sticking problems.

Before You Start:

Tools & Materials: screwdriver, hammer, spray solvent/lubricant, wooden golf tees or dowels, carpenter's glue, sandpaper, wood sealer.

Tip: Lubricate the hinge pins to eliminate squeaking in doors.

Tip: To tighten hinge screws without removing the door, block up the bottom of door with wood shims.

How to Remove a Door

1 Drive the lower hinge pin out with a screwdriver and hammer. Have a helper hold door in place. Drive out the upper hinge pin.

2 Remove the door and set it aside. Before replacing the door, clean and lubricate all the hinge pins.

How to Tighten Loose Hinges

1 Remove door from hinges (page opposite). Tighten any loose screws. If wood behind hinge will not hold screws, remove hinges.

2 Coat wooden golf tees or dowels with glue and drive them into worn screw holes. Let glue dry. Cut off excess wood.

3 Drill pilot holes in new wood. Rehang hinge with new wood as base for screws.

How to Fix a Sticking Door

1 Tighten any loose hinges (above). If sticking problem continues, use light pencil lines to mark areas where the door sticks.

2 During dry weather, remove door (page opposite). Sand or plane marked areas until door fits. Seal ends and edges with clear wood sealer before rehanging door.

Cutting Off an Interior Door

Prehung interior doors are sized to allow a ¾-inch gap between the bottom of the door and the floor. This gap lets the door swing without binding on the carpet or floorcovering. If thicker carpeting or a larger threshold is installed, a small portion of the door may need to be cut off with a circular saw.

Wider cuts may be needed if a door is altered to fit a special installation, like in a child's room or an undersized storage closet.

Hollow-core interior doors have a solid wood frame, with centers that are hollow. If the entire bottom frame member is cut away when shortening the door, it can be reinserted to close the hollow door cavity.

Before You Start:
Tools & Materials: tape measure, hammer, screwdriver, utility knife, sawhorses, circular saw and straightedge, chisel, carpenter's glue, clamps.

Tip: Measure carefully when marking a door for cutting. Measure from the top of the carpeting, not from the floor.

How to Cut Off an Interior Door

1 With door in place, measure ⅜" up from top of floorcovering and mark door. Remove door from the hinges by removing the hinge pins.

2 Mark cutting line. Cut through door veneer with sharp utility knife to prevent it from chipping when the door is sawed.

3 Lay door on sawhorses. Clamp a straightedge to the door as a cutting guide.

4 Saw off bottom of the door. The hollow core of the door may be exposed.

5 To replace a cut-off frame in the bottom of the door, chisel the veneer from both sides of the removed portion.

6 Apply wood glue to cut-off frame. Insert frame into opening, and clamp. Wipe away excess glue and let dry overnight.

Removing & Replacing an Entry Door

Replacing a warped, leaky entry door is a relatively easy project. New, energy-efficient entry doors come prehung with jambs and all installation hardware, except locks. Steel replacement doors will not warp or peel, are fully insulated and weatherstripped, and are more secure than wooden doors.

Before You Start:
Tools & Materials: tape measure, hammer, screwdriver, Wonderbar®, utility knife, silicone caulk, caulk gun, wood shims, carpenter's level, 16d galvanized nails, door lockset.

How to Remove & Replace an Entry Door

1 Measure height and width of existing door. Purchase replacement door to match measurements. Drive out hinge pins with hammer and screwdriver. Remove door.

2 Use a pry bar and hammer to gently remove interior door trim. Save trim to reapply after new door is installed.

Brick molding

3 Use a utility knife to cut away old caulk between the exterior siding and the brick molding on the door frame.

4 Pry away and discard old door jamb and threshold. Stubborn nails can be cut with a reciprocating saw.

(continued next page)

5 Place door unit into rough opening and check fit. There should be about ⅜-inch space on sides and top. Remove door unit.

6 Apply caulk to new threshold to form weather seal between the threshold and floor. Place door unit in rough opening.

Jamb

7 Tap wood shims (filler strips) into gaps between frame and jambs until level shows unit is plumb. Insert shims at lockset and all hinge locations.

8 Nail through jambs and shims into framing members with 16d casing nails. Check for plumb after driving each nail.

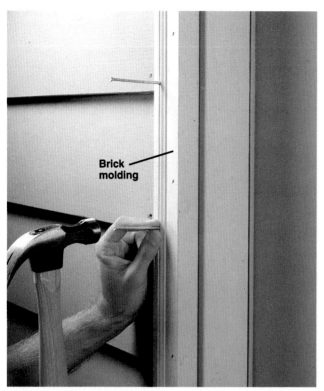

9 Drive 16d galvanized casing nails through brick molding into door frame.

10 Replace casing on inside of door jamb. If trim was damaged during removal, cut and install new casing.

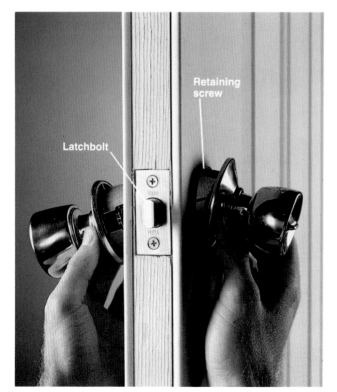

11 Install new door lock. First, insert the latchbolt mechanism through latchbolt hole. Then insert the lockset tailpieces through latchbolt, and screw the handles together by tightening retaining screws.

12 Screw the strike plate to the door jamb and adjust the plate position to fit the latchbolt. Caulk any gaps between siding and new door molding.

Walls & Ceilings

Walls & Ceilings

Materials for Walls & Ceilings

Fiberglass joint tape

Repair patch

Replacement tiles

Wall hangers

Sandpaper

The most common problems with walls and ceilings include holes, structural cracks, stains and water damage. Repairs to wallboard walls are the easiest, because damaged sections can be readily removed and replaced. But if you have plaster construction, check the overall condition of the walls and ceiling before making repairs. If the whole surface feels spongy, or if the bulges or cracks are extensive, the paster should be covered or replaced by a professional.

For most wall and ceiling repairs, choose a pre-mixed patching plaster or taping compound that combines easy application and no-mess cleanup. There are also many water-based products available for working on walls and ceilings that are easier and safer for you to use.

Tips for Walls & Ceilings

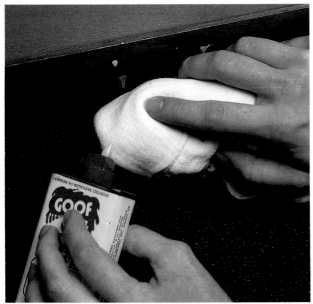

Latex paint spatters can be removed from most surfaces with a solvent cleaner. Test on an inconspicuous area before using it on stains.

Seal stains which bleed through paint, like lipstick, ink, oil and rust. Spray or brush clear shellac over stain. Let shellac dry completely before repainting surface.

Grout float

Adhesive trowel

Wallboard saw

Utility knife

Heat gun

Wallcovering roller

Awl

Sash brush

Wallboard knives

Glue gun

Adhesive syringe

Magnetic stud finder

Tile nippers

Tools for Walls & Ceilings

How to Remove Stains from Walls & Ceilings

1 Test stain and graffiti removers on an inconspicuous area. Some products may alter paint or wallcovering dyes.

2 Spray stain remover directly on clean cloth. Dab stain area with stain remover.

3 Wipe or blot the stain area with a clean, dry cloth. With stubborn stains, rub gently with a fiber scrub brush or pad.

Fastening Objects to Walls or Ceilings

Light and medium wall loads can be supported by plaster or wallboard, but heavy loads, such as bookshelves, should be anchored to studs or joists.

Studs are placed at uniform intervals of 16 or 24 inches on center: after finding one stud, measure equal distances to find the others.

When hanging some objects, such as drapery rods, there may not be a stud where you need one. To hang objects between studs, select a wall fastener designed for your type of walls and rated for the intended weight load. Fastener packages list acceptable weight loads.

Before You Start:

Tools & Materials: magnetic or electronic stud finder, wall fasteners, drill and bits, hammer, screwdriver.

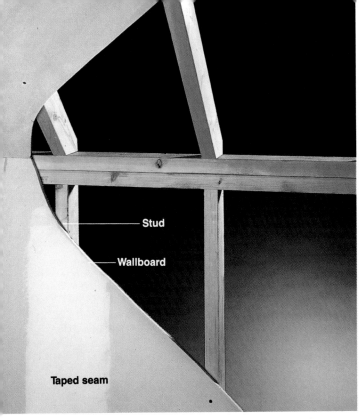

Stud

Wallboard

Taped seam

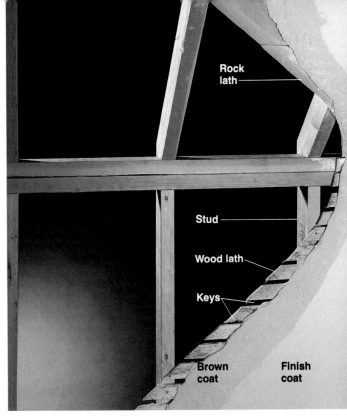

Rock lath

Stud

Wood lath

Keys

Brown coat

Finish coat

Wallboard construction, also known as drywall, uses gypsum panels nailed or screwed directly to framing members. Wallboard thickness varies from ¼" to ⅝". The studs or joists behind a wallboard surface are usually 16" or 24" apart, measured "on center." You can use a wide variety of wall fasteners in wallboard.

Plaster construction is applied in layers. Behind the plaster is a layer of wood, metal or rock lath which holds the plaster in place. Keys, formed when the base plaster is squeezed through the lath, hold the dried plaster to the walls and ceilings. Because plaster is a brittle surface, always drill pilot holes when hanging objects. Use screw-type fasteners whenever possible.

How to Find a Stud or Joist for Heavy Loads

Nail holes

Nail location

Check for nails on baseboard trim, indicating stud locations. Studs are also found next to door and window frames, and along electrical outlets or light fixtures, and furnace ducts.

Use a lamp with shade removed. Sidelighting the wall with other lights turned off will reveal indentations caused by nail or screw heads attached to studs.

Use magnetic or electronic stud finder to locate steel nails. Work stud finder over the wall randomly until the magnet indicates a nail in a stud.

How to Hang Lightweight Objects Between Studs

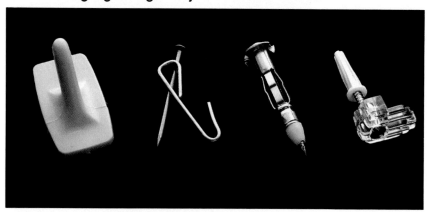

Wallhangers for light loads, from left: adhesive hook (for very light loads on untextured walls), nailed picture hanger hook, drivable molly bolt, plastic anchor with attached mirror clip.

1 Hang lightweight mirror by mounting 2 mirror clips for each corner of mirror. You will need mirror clips, plastic anchors, drill and bits.

How to Hang Mediumweight Objects Between Studs

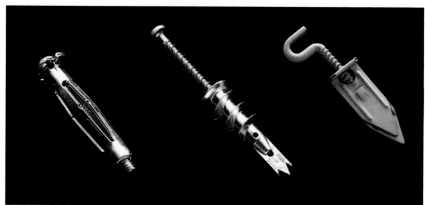

Wallhangers for medium loads, from left: molly bolt with sleeve (available in various diameters and lengths), Grip-It™ screw anchor with wallboard twist anchor, drivable wall anchor.

1 Hang mediumweight drapes using Grip-It screws when there is no wall stud. You will need drapery brackets and Grip-It screw kit.

How to Hang Heavy Objects Between Studs or Joists

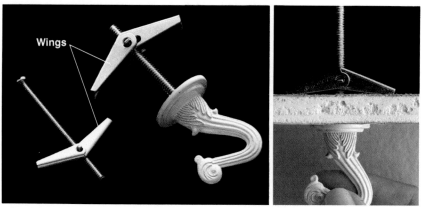

Wallhangers for heavy loads, from left: toggle bolt, headless toggle bolt with hook. Spring-loaded wings on toggle bolt collapse to fit through drilled hole, then spring open to brace against wall or ceiling as bolt is tightened.

1 Hang heavy plants using head-less toggle bolt with hook. You will need drill and bit, toggle bolt with hook.

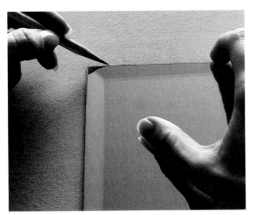

2 Hold mirror against wall, and mark corner edges of mirror with light pencil. Mark location of screw holes for mirror clips.

3 Select bit with diameter equal to plastic anchor. Drill holes with masonry bit and drive in plastic anchors.

4 Screw in bottom mirror clips. Mount mirror inside clips. Attach remaining clips.

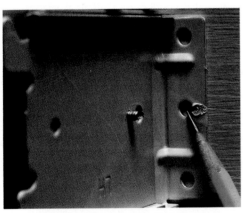

2 Measure length of drapes to determine height of brackets. Mark location of screw holes for brackets.

Twist anchor

3 Tap twist anchors into wallboard, then screw them in. If mounting on plaster, drill pilot holes for Grip-It screws.

Screw anchor

4 Mount drapery brackets by driving Grip-It screw anchor into twist anchor or drilled plaster. Hang drapes.

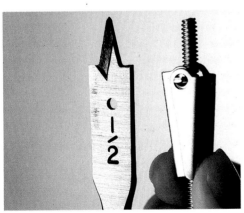

2 Select bit with diameter equal to collapsed wings of toggle bolt. Drill hole in ceiling.

3 Insert collapsed toggle bolt into hole until wings spring open. Pull bolt down slightly.

4 Attach ceiling hook to toggle bolt. Turn hook while pulling slightly, until bolt and hook are tight.

Preparing & Repairing Walls & Ceilings

Thoroughly washing, rinsing and sanding your walls before priming will guarantee a long-lasting finish. For a professional appearance, carefully check your walls for damage and repair the wallboard or plaster as needed. Pregummed fiberglass repair tapes and premixed patching compounds reduce drying time and let you patch and paint a wall the same day.

Wash and sand before repainting. Use TSP (trisodium phosphate) solution and a sponge to cut grease and to remove dirt. Wear rubber gloves, and wash walls from the bottom up with a damp sponge to avoid streaks. Rinse thoroughly with clean water. After drying, sand surfaces lightly.

How to Remove Stains

1 Apply stain remover to a clean, dry cloth, and rub lightly to remove the stain.

2 Seal all stain areas with white pigmented shellac. Pigmented shellac prevents stains from bleeding through the new paint.

Water or rust stains may indicate water damage. Check for leaking pipes and soft plaster, make needed repairs, then seal area with stain-killing sealer.

How to Remove Mildew

1 Test stains by washing with water and detergent. Mildew stains will not wash out.

2 Wearing rubber gloves and eye protection, wash the walls with bleach, which kills mildew spores.

3 After bleach treatment, wash mildew away with TSP solution, and rinse with clear water.

How to Patch Peeling Paint

1 Scrape away loose paint with a putty knife or paint scraper.

2 Apply spackle to the edges of chipped paint with a putty knife or flexible wallboard knife.

3 Sand the patch area with 150-grit production sandpaper. Patch area should feel smooth to the touch.

Repairing Holes in Plaster

Modern repair methods and materials have simplified the job of repairing holes in plaster. Coating the patch area with latex bonding liquid ensures a good bond and a tight, crack-free patch. Bonding liquid also eliminates the need to wet the plaster and lath to prevent premature drying and shrinkage. Ask your hardware dealer for a good concrete/plaster latex bonding liquid.

How to Repair Holes in Plaster

1 Sand or scrape any textured paint from the area around the hole.

2 Test with a scraper to be sure plaster is solid and tight around the damaged area. Scrape away any loose or soft plaster.

3 Apply latex bonding liquid liberally around edges of hole and over base lath to ensure crack-free bond between old and new plaster.

4 Mix patching plaster as directed by manufacturer, and use a wallboard knife or trowel to apply it to the hole. Fill shallow holes with a single coat of plaster.

5 For deeper holes, apply shallow first coat, then scratch crosshatch pattern in wet plaster. Let dry, then apply second coat of plaster. Let dry, and sand lightly.

Use texture paint or wallboard compound to recreate any surface texture.

How to Fill Nail Holes

1 Apply lightweight spackle to the hole with a putty knife or your fingertip. This keeps repair area small so it is easy to hide with paint. Let spackle dry.

2 Sand the repair area lightly with 150-grit production sandpaper. Production paper has an open surface that does not clog. Wipe dust away with a damp sponge, then prime the spot with PVA primer.

How to Fill Shallow Dents & Holes

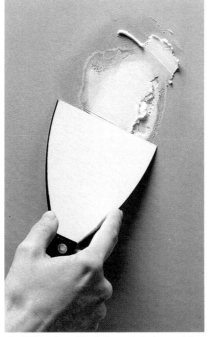

1 Scrape or sand away any loose plaster, peeled paint or wallboard face paper to ensure a solid base for patching.

2 Fill hole with lightweight spackle. Apply spackle with smallest wallboard knife that will span the entire hole. Let spackle dry.

3 Sand lightly with 150-grit production sandpaper.

How to Fix Popped Wallboard Nails

1 Drive wallboard screw 2" away from popped nail. Be sure the screw hits the stud or joist and pulls the wallboard tight against the framing.

2 Scrape away loose paint or wallboard compound. Drive the popped nail back into the framing so the head is sunk 1/32" below the surface of the wallboard. Do not set the nail with a punch.

3 Use wallboard knife to apply 3 coats of premixed wallboard compound to nail and screw holes. Allow drying time after each coat. Compound will shrink. Sand and spot-prime the patch area.

How to Repair Cracks in Plaster

1 Scrape away any texture or loose plaster around the crack. Reinforce crack with pregummed fiberglass wallboard tape.

2 Use taping knife or trowel to apply spackle or wallboard compound over tape so that tape is just concealed: if compound is too thick, it will recrack.

3 Apply a second thin coat if necessary to conceal the tape edges. Sand lightly and prime the repair area. Retexture the surface.

How to Patch Small Holes in Wallboard

1 Inspect the damaged area. If there are no cracks around the edge of the hole, just fill the hole with spackle, let dry and sand it smooth.

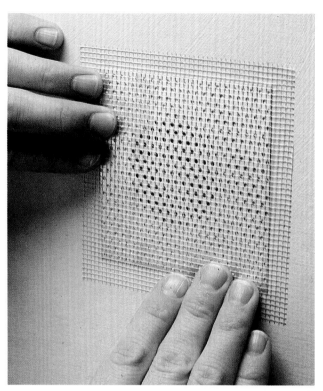

2 If edges are cracked, cover hole with peel-and-stick repair patch. The patch has a metal mesh center for strength, and can be cut or shaped as needed. Patches are available in several sizes.

3 Use wallboard knife to cover patch with spackle or wallboard compound. Two coats may be needed. Let patch set until nearly dry.

4 Use a damp sponge or wallboard wet sander to smooth the repair area. This eliminates dust caused by dry sanding.

How to Patch Larger Holes in Wallboard

1 Outline the damaged area with a carpenter's square. Use a wallboard saw or jig saw to cut away the damaged section.

2 Install wood or wallboard backer strips. For wood, use a wallboard screw gun and 1¼'' wallboard screws to secure the strip in place.

3 Or, use wallboard backers secured by hot glue as an alternative to wood backer strips. Screw or glue wallboard patch in place over backer strips.

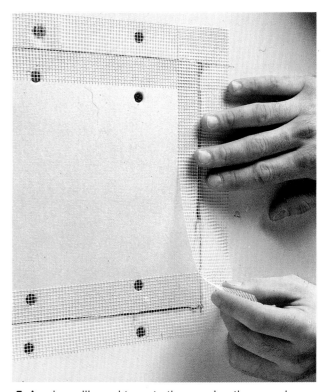

4 Apply wallboard tape to the cracks, then apply wallboard compound and sand the area (page opposite).

Installing Wallboard

Wallboard is commonly available in 4 × 8- and 4 × 12-foot sheets, and in thicknesses ranging from ⅜ to ¾ inch. For easy handling in most applications, use 4 × 8-foot sheets of ½-inch-thick wallboard. For extra fire protection where building codes require it, or for soundproofing walls and ceilings, use ⅝-inch wallboard.

Install wallboard with wallboard nails and a wallboard hammer. Wallboard can also be installed with panel adhesive and wallboard screws. Adhesives bridge minor framing problems, and provide a smooth, easy-to-finish surface that is not subject to nail pops.

Wallboard panels are tapered along the long edges, so that adjoining panels form a slightly recessed seam that can be easily covered with paper tape and wallboard joint compound. Panels joined end-to-end are difficult to finish, so avoid end-butted seams wherever possible.

Before You Start:

Tools & Materials: straightedge, hammer, 4 x 8-foot wallboard panels, tape measure, wallboard T-square, utility knife, wallboard saw, jig saw, circle cutter, sawhorse scaffolding (page 52), wallboard hammer, wallboard nails, screwgun, 1¼-inch wallboard screws, wallboard lifter, panel adhesive, caulk gun.

Tip: Inspect wallboard panels for broken corners and cracks before installation. Damaged wallboard is difficult to install, and causes finishing problems.

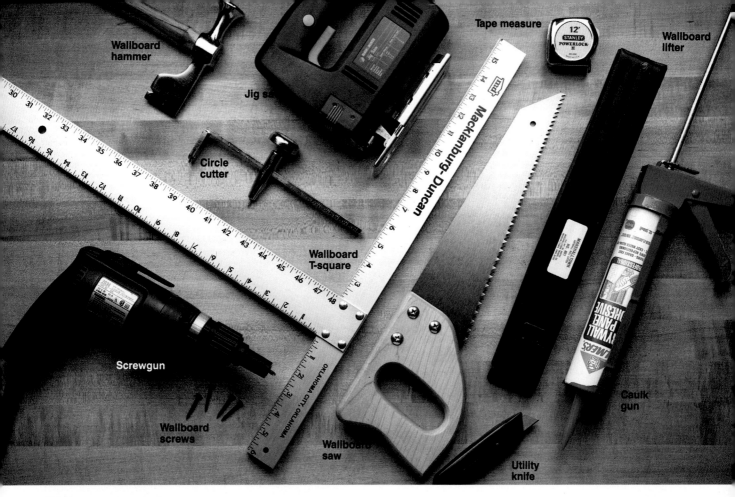

Wallboard installation tools include: wallboard hammer with convex head for indenting nail heads, jig saw, tape measure, wallboard lifter for positioning wallboard panels, caulk gun and panel adhesive, utility knife, wallboard saw for straight cuts around windows and doors, wallboard T-square, wallboard screws, screwgun with adjustable clutch for adjusting screw depth, circle cutter for making round cutouts for wall lighting fixtures.

How to Prepare for Wallboard Installation

1 Check stud alignment with straightedge that is at least 4' long. Remove and replace any warped studs.

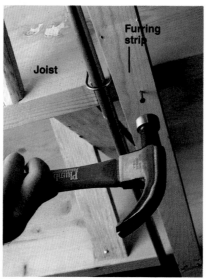

2 Check for obstructions, like water pipes or heating ducts that hang below joists. Nail furring strips to framing to extend wall surface, or move obstructions.

3 Mark locations of studs with carpenter's pencil or masking tape on floor. Wallboard will cover studs, so these marks show where to nail.

How to Cut Wallboard

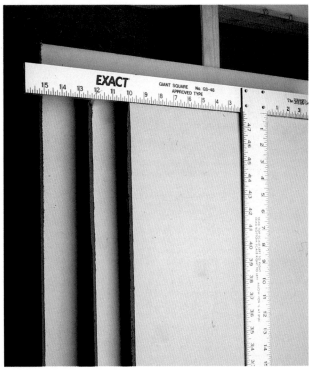

1 Set wallboard upright with smooth side out when cutting panels. Cut and install wallboard panels one at a time.

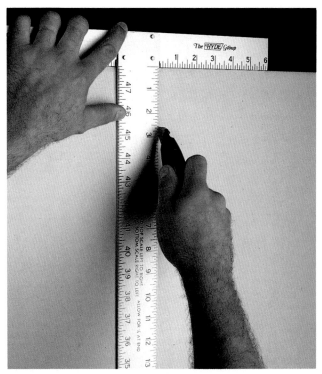

2 Use tape measure to measure length needed. Position wallboard T-square with short arm flush against edge. Use a utility knife to score wallboard face paper along long arm of square.

3 Bend scored section with both hands to break plaster core of wallboard. Fold back unwanted piece. Cut through back paper to separate pieces.

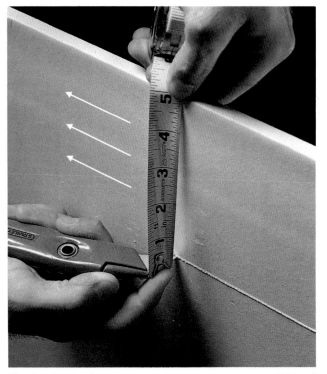

For horizontal cuts, extend tape measure to width of desired cut, and hook utility knife blade under end of tape. Hold tape tightly in one hand, utility knife tightly in other hand. Move both hands along panel to score a cut in face paper.

How to Cut Notches and Openings in Wallboard

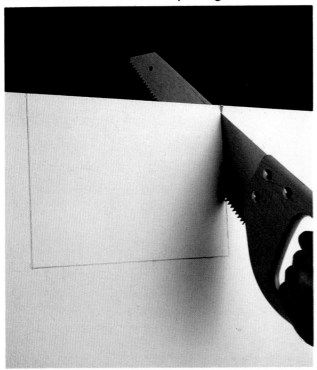

1 Use a wallboard saw to cut shortest sides of notch. A wallboard saw has coarse, wide-set teeth that cuts quickly without clogging.

2 Use a utility knife to cut remaining side of notch, then break plaster core as shown. Cut back paper with utility knife to separate unwanted portion.

Cut openings for electrical and telephone outlets, and heating ducts, by making plunge cuts with a jig saw and coarse, wood-cutting blade (page 23).

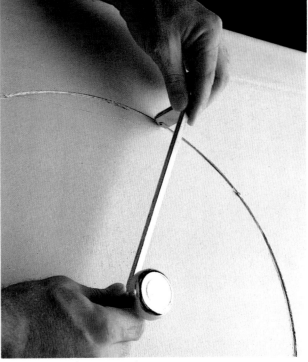

Make circular cutouts for light fixtures or exhaust fans with an adjustable circle cutter. Mark a center point and use the circle cutter to score both sides of wallboard. Tap with a hammer to release cutout from surrounding panel.

How to Install Wallboard Ceilings

1 Install wallboard panels on ceiling before installing wall panels. Mark ceiling joist locations on top plate as a nailing guide for installing wallboard. Always work with a partner when installing wallboard ceilings.

2 Place a sponge in work cap before installing wallboard on ceiling. Sponge provides cushion while worker uses head to hold panel in place for nailing.

3 Build a scaffold out of sawhorses and lumber so the top of worker's head just touches bottom of ceiling joists. Use head to hold panel while it is nailed.

4 Apply panel adhesive to bottom of joists. Hold wallboard tightly against joists with top of head. This frees hands for nailing or screwing wallboard.

How to Install Wallboard Walls

1 Attach wallboard with panel adhesive and wallboard screws. Apply adhesive to studs with caulk gun. At joints, apply adhesive in a wavy pattern so both panel edges contact it.

2 Install wallboard panels vertically to avoid butt joints that are difficult to finish. Lift panels tight against ceiling with wallboard lifter, then screw panels into position.

3 Drive 1¼-inch wallboard screws through panel into studs with screwgun. Follow screw interval recommended by manufacturer.

4 Plan wallboard placement so there are no joints at corners of doors or windows. Wallboard joints at corners often crack and cause bulges that interfere with miter joints in window or door trim.

Finishing Wallboard

To finish wallboard, apply wallboard compound to all seams, nail and screw holes, and corners. Because wallboard compound shrinks as it dries, three coats are needed to compensate for shrinkage. Apply the first coat with a 4- or 6-inch taping knife and let dry thoroughly. Apply the last two coats with a 10-inch knife.

To prevent cracking, all joints must be reinforced. On outside corners, nail metal corners over the wallboard before applying compound. On inside corners and flat joints, apply a thin first layer of compound, then press strips of paper wallboard tape into the damp compound.

Wallboard finishing tools include: plastic mud pan with metal edges for holding wallboard taping compound; wallboard wet sander for smoothing wallboard joints without raising dust; 4-, 6-, and 10-inch-wide wallboard knives; pole sander for sanding in high corners.

Tip: To avoid dust, use a wallboard wet sander instead of sandpaper to smooth joints.

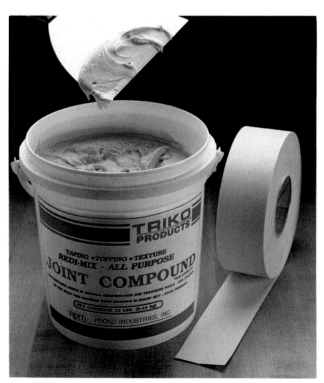

Use premixed wallboard compound for most taping and finishing jobs, to eliminate messy mixing. Use paper wallboard tape when using premixed wallboard compound.

For small projects, use quick-set wallboard compound that is mixed with water. Quick-set compound hardens in 1 to 2 hours. Use fiberglass wallboard tape when using quick-set compound.

How to Tape Wallboard Joints

1 Apply a thin layer of wallboard compound over joint with a 4- or 6-inch wallboard knife. To load knife, dip it into mud pan filled with wallboard compound.

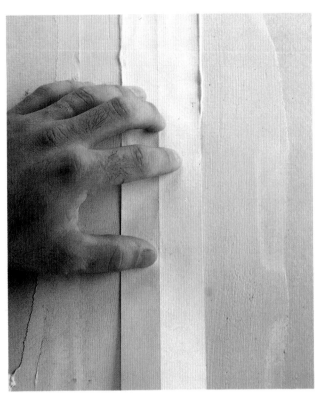

2 Press wallboard tape into compound immediately, centering tape on joint. Wipe away excess compound and smooth joint with 6-inch knife. Let dry.

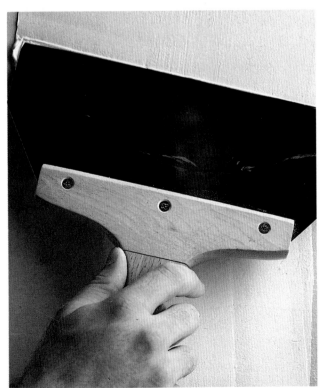

3 Apply 2 thin finish coats of compound with 10-inch wallboard knife. Allow second coat to dry and shrink overnight before applying last coat. Let the last coat harden slightly before wet-sanding.

4 Smooth the finish coat with wallboard wet sander before compound dries completely. Wet sander smooths compound without raising plaster dust.

How to Finish Inside Corners

1 Fold a strip of paper wallboard tape in half by pinching the strip and pulling it between thumb and forefinger.

2 Apply thin layer of premixed wallboard compound to both sides of the inside corner, using a 4-inch wallboard knife.

3 Position end of folded tape strip at top of corner joint. Press tape into wet compound with wallboard knife, and smooth both sides of corner.

4 Apply second coat of compound to one side of corner at a time. When first side of corner is dry, finish opposite corner. After second coat dries, apply final coat of compound. Smooth final coat with wet sander (page 103).

How to Finish Outside Corners

1 Position steel corner bead on outside corners. Using a level, adjust bead so corner is plumb. Nail into place with 1¼-inch wallboard nails spaced at 8-inch intervals.

2 Cover corner bead with 3 coats of wallboard compound, using 6- or 10-inch wallboard knife. Let each coat dry and shrink overnight before applying next coat. Smooth final coat with wet sander (page 103).

How to Finish Nails & Screws

Cover screw or nail heads with 3 coats of wallboard compound, using a 4- or 6-inch wallboard knife. Allow each coat to dry overnight before applying next coat.

How to Sand Joints

Sand joints lightly after wallboard compound dries. Use pole sander to reach high areas without a ladder. Wear a dust mask when dry-sanding.

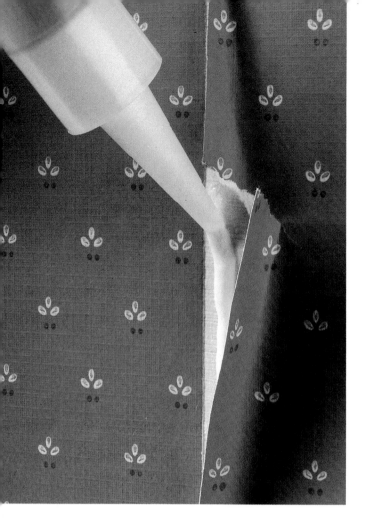

Repairing Wallcoverings

Damage to wallcoverings may require that you cut and install a patch. Loosened seams and bubbles are common wallcovering problems. Although new vinyls make modern wallcoverings more durable than older "paper" coverings, occasionally they need repair. Removing stains is much easier with new vinyl surfaces.

Before You Start:

Tools & Materials: adhesive and applicator, roller, wallpaper dough, shellac, wallcovering remnants, utility knife, sponge.

Tip: Save wallcovering remnants for future repairs, or remove patch section from an inconspicuous spot, such as a closet or behind a door.

Tips for Wallcoverings

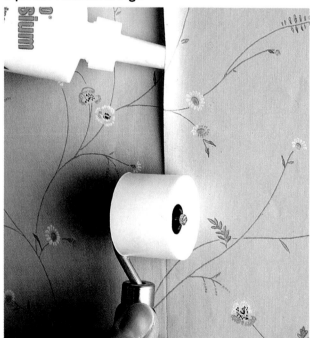

To fix seams, lift edge of wallcovering and insert tip of glue applicator under it. Squirt adhesive onto the wall. Press edge back in place with a roller and wipe away excess adhesive with a clean, wet sponge.

Clean soiled wallcovering with wallpaper dough or a gum eraser, purchased from your decorating center.

How to Patch Wallcoverings

1 Fasten wallcovering patch material to the wall over the damaged portion with removable tape, so that the pattern aligns with the existing wallcovering.

2 Cut through both layers of wallcovering with a sharp knife to assure a perfect pattern match. Remove patch material, then apply water to damaged area of wallcovering.

3 Peel the damaged section away from the wall. Apply adhesive to the back of the patch and carefully position it in the hole so patterns match. Wipe with a clean wet sponge.

How to Flatten Bubbles

1 Cut a slit at the edge of the bubble using a utility knife. If there is a pattern in the covering, cut along a pattern line to help conceal the cut.

2 Insert tip of glue applicator under flap and apply adhesive sparingly to the wall underneath the covering.

3 Press gently to rebond the wallcovering. Use a clean wet sponge to press the flap down and wipe away excess adhesive.

Ceramic Tile Care & Repair

Ceramic tile is durable and nearly maintenance-free, but the grout between the tiles can deteriorate. Damaged grout offers the only point of water entry, and water penetration will destroy the tile base, and eventually, the entire tile job.

To avoid stains and mineral buildup on tiles, use a bath towel to wipe down the tile walls after using the bath or shower. Use an exhaust fan to remove humid air and avoid mildew and moisture damage.

Before You Start:

Tools & Materials: 3/8" variable-speed drill, carbide bit, masonry anchor, hammer, chisel, utility knife, replacement tile, tile adhesive, masking tape, grout, rubbing alcohol, awl, tub caulk.

Tip: Ceramic tile that dates before the 1960s was set in a masonry base, and repairs should be done by a professional. Remember to use protective eyewear whenever using a hammer and chisel.

How to Hang Tile Fixtures

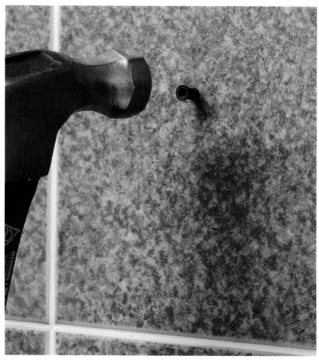

1 Place masking tape over the spot where you want to drill. Drill hole for anchor using a carbide masonry bit and 3/8-inch variable-speed drill. Drill bit should be same size as anchor. Use low drill speed to ensure that bit does not skip on tile.

2 Tap a plastic or lead masonry anchor plug into the hole and use a screw to attach the fixture. Be careful not to chip the tile.

How to Remove & Replace Broken Tiles

1 Scrape away old grout from between the tiles with a utility knife or awl. Break tile into small pieces with a chisel and hammer for easy removal. Scrape debris and old adhesive from hole with a utility knife or sharp scraper.

2 Test-fit new tile to be sure it sits flush with the old tile. Spread adhesive on the back of the replacement tile. Place tile in the hole and twist slightly to ensure contact with wall. Use masking tape to hold tile in place overnight.

Sponge

3 Remove the masking tape. Apply premixed tile grout with a sponge or grout float. Let grout set slightly, then wipe away excess with damp cloth.

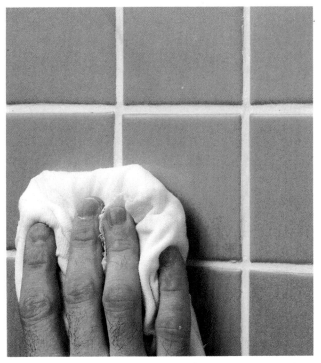

4 Let grout dry for about 1 hour. Polish the tile with a clean dry cloth to remove the powdery residue.

How to Regrout Ceramic Tile

1 Scrape out old grout with an awl or utility knife to leave a clean bed for the new grout. Remove and replace any broken tiles (page 109).

2 Clean and rinse the grout joints with a sponge. Choose premixed grout that is resistant to mildew and stains.

3 Use a foam grout float or sponge to spread grout over entire tile surface. Work grout well into joints. Let grout set slightly, until firm, then wipe away the excess with a damp cloth.

4 Let grout dry completely. Wipe away powdery residue and polish the tiles with a dry soft cloth. Apply caulk around bathtub or shower stall (page opposite). Do not use tub or shower for 24 hours.

How to Recaulk Around a Bathtub or Shower Stall

1 Scrape out old grout or caulk with an awl or can opener. Wipe away soap scum from joint with rubbing alcohol and a clean cloth.

2 Fill tub with water so it will be heavy enough to pull tub away from the tile. Fill joint with a silicone or latex caulk that will not become brittle.

3 Wet your fingertip with cold water so the caulk will not stick to your finger, and smooth the caulk into a cove shape. Let caulk harden and trim any excess away with a utility knife.

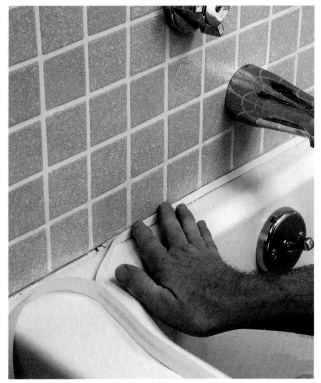

Peel-and-stick tub & tile caulks are pre-formed, reducing the work of cleaning the joint and cleaning up the new caulk. Peel the backing off and press the new caulk into place.

How to Prepare Woodwork for Painting

1 Wash woodwork with TSP solution, and rinse. Scrape away any peeling or loose paint. Badly chipped woodwork should be stripped.

How to Prepare Varnished Wood for Refinishing

1 Clean woodwork with a soft cloth and odorless mineral spirits or liquid furniture refinisher.

Cleaning & Patching Woodwork

For the best results, woodwork should be cleaned, patched and sanded before it is repainted. A liquid deglosser helps to dull shiny surfaces so they will bond with new paint. If new hardware is to be installed, check to see if new pieces will fit old screw holes. If new screw holes must be drilled, fill the old holes with wood patch.

To renew varnished wood, clean the surfaces with mineral spirits or furniture refinisher, then patch holes with a wood patcher that is tinted to match the existing finish. Sand wood smooth, and apply one or two coats of varnish.

2 Use a putty knife to apply latex wood patch or spackle to any nail holes, dents, and to any other damaged areas.

3 Sand surfaces with 150-grit production paper until they are smooth to the touch. Wipe woodwork with a tack cloth before priming and painting.

2 Apply wood patch to holes and dents with putty knife. Sand patch areas lightly with 150-grit production sandpaper.

3 Restain the patch areas to match surrounding wood. Apply 1 or 2 coats of varnish.

Floors

Floor Repairs

The most common floor repairs include removing burns or stains from carpet or hardwood, replacing or repairing damaged vinyl, restoring damaged or stained hardwood, and silencing floors and stairs that squeak.

If you saved the leftovers from a floorcovering installation, you already have the materials needed to repair small areas of damaged vinyl or carpeting. If you do not have remnants, take patch material from an inconspicuous area — a carpeted closet, or the tiled area behind a kitchen appliance.

Rental stores have floor tools such as power stretchers, glue irons for refastening loose carpet seams and carpet edge trimmers. Describe the problem, and ask the rental clerk to suggest the right tools for your project.

Tools and Materials for Floor Repair

Tips for Carpet Care

Prevent damage and excessive wear on your floors by placing a door mat at each entry. The mat prevents tracking grit onto floors, reducing wear and cleaning.

Choose a powerful vacuum sweeper such as this upright model to ensure deep-down carpet cleaning power. Grit in carpet fibers causes premature wear.

Repairing Carpeting

Stains and burns are the most common carpeting problems. If you cannot remove a stain, you usually can patch the carpeting by cutting away the damaged area and inserting a new piece of carpet. With superficial burns, clip away burned fibers with a fingernail scissors.

Another common problem is carpet seams or edges that have come loose. You can rent tools for fixing all of the problems shown on these pages.

Before You Start:

Tools & Materials: cookie-cutter carpet tool, double-face tape, knee kicker, seam adhesive, heat-activated tape, seam iron.

How to Repair Burned or Stained Carpeting

1 Remove extensive damage or stain with "cookie-cutter" tool, available at carpeting stores. Press cutter down over damaged area and twist to cut away carpet.

2 Cut replacement patch from scrap carpeting using cookie cutter. Insert double-face carpet tape under carpet so that tape overlaps patch seam.

3 Press patch into place. Make sure direction of nap or pattern matches existing carpet. Seal seam with seam adhesive to prevent unraveling.

How to Restretch Loose Carpeting

1 Adjust head of knee kicker so that prongs reach through to carpet backing. Press head of kicker into carpet about 2 inches from wall.

2 Press firmly with knee to stretch carpeting over and down onto tackless strip. Tuck carpeting over strip with putty knife. If necessary, trim excess carpeting. Carpet backing is held by points on strip.

How to Reglue Loose Seams

1 Remove old tape from under carpet seam. Cut new heat-activated carpet tape to fit seam. Place tape under carpeting so that both carpet edges over-lap tape.

2 Seal seam using a rented seam iron. Run heated iron along tape under carpeting to activate glue. As iron moves along, press down on seam to seal edges of carpet.

Repairing Vinyl Floorcovering

Deep scratches or tears in vinyl floorcoverings can usually be repaired if you have a patch that matches the damaged vinyl. Patterned floorcoverings like simulated brick or stone are easy to repair, because the edges of the patch are concealed by the pattern. If necessary, remove vinyl from a hidden area to use as patch material.

Before You Start:

Tools & Materials: scrap floorcovering, masking tape, carpenter's square, utility knife, putty knife, odorless mineral spirits, floorcovering adhesive, roller (rolling pin will do).

Tip: When selecting new floorcovering, select true inlaid material, usually sold in 6-foot wide rolls. It is heavier and much more resistant to wear and damage than lighter vinyls.

How to Repair Vinyl Floorcovering

1 Select scrap vinyl that matches existing floor. Place the scrap over the damaged area and adjust it until the pattern matches. Tape the patch to the floor.

2 Use carpenter's square to outline patch. Draw along pattern lines to conceal patch seams. Use utility knife to cut through both layers of vinyl. Lift out damaged vinyl with a putty knife.

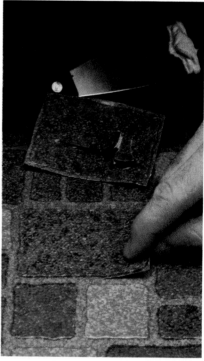

3 Apply mineral spirits to dissolve adhesive, then scrape clean with a putty knife or razor scraper. Apply new adhesive to patch, then fit patch into hole. Use roller on vinyl to ensure good bond. Wipe away excess adhesive.

Replacing Vinyl Floor Tiles

Replace individual floor tiles when they become buckled, cracked, or when they are badly stained. If you cannot find replacement tiles at a home center, remove a tile from a hidden area, inside a closet or behind a kitchen appliance.

Older tiles made of asphalt may have asbestos fibers in the backing. Because asbestos poses a health risk, have a professional replace the floorcovering.

Before You Start:

Tools & Materials: heat gun, odorless mineral spirits, putty knife, replacement floor tile, floor-covering adhesive, notched trowel, roller (rolling pin will do).

Tip: If you do not have a heat gun, try setting a pan of ice cubes over the tile. The cold makes the tile adhesive brittle, allowing the tile to pop up easily.

How to Replace Vinyl Floor Tiles

1 Use a heat gun to heat tile and soften underlying adhesive. Be careful not to melt tile. Lift tile out with putty knife.

2 Apply mineral spirits to dissolve floorcovering adhesive. Scrape away all adhesive with putty knife or razor scraper.

3 Apply adhesive to underlayment. Position tile in hole. Use roller on tile to ensure a good bond. Wipe away excess adhesive.

Repairing Hardwood Floors

Repair scratches and holes in hardwood floors with a latex wood patch (available in various wood tones), and remove stains with oxalic acid, available at home centers or paint stores. For routine cleaning and renewing, choose a hardwood floor kit containing wood cleaner, restorer and application cloth.

Give hardwood a coat of protective wax/cleaner twice yearly to guard against scratches and water damage. Always use solvent-type cleaners on hardwood: water-base cleaners can blacken wood.

Before You Start:

Tools & Materials: wood patch, putty knife, sandpaper, wood restorer, rubber gloves, oxalic acid, vinegar, wood cleaner, combination wax/cleaner.

Tip: If your floors have excessive wax buildup, strip them with odorless mineral spirits, then rewax with a solvent-type wax/cleaner.

How to Patch Hardwood Floors

1 Apply a latex wood patch to fill in the scratches, staple marks or nail holes in hardwood floors.

2 Sand the wood patch smooth with fine sandpaper. Sand in the direction of wood grain.

3 Apply wood restorer with a clean cloth, and blend it into the existing finish.

How to Remove Stains from Hardwood Floors

1 Sand the stain area to remove old finish. Wearing rubber gloves, pour oxalic acid on stain and let stand for one hour to bleach stain. Repeat if necessary.

2 Rinse the stain area with vinegar. Let the wood dry completely.

3 Coat the bleached wood with a wood restorer. Apply several coats of restorer until the floor matches the old finish.

How to Clean & Renew Hardwood Floors

1 Vacuum hardwood floor to remove grit and dirt. Pour wood cleaner from kit on worn areas. When renewing an entire room, divide floor into 3 × 3-foot sections.

2 Rub over area with a dry cloth or fine steel wool. Let floor dry, then buff the wood by hand or with a buffing machine.

3 Apply a combination wax/ cleaner or paste wax, then wax twice yearly for extra protection.

Floor boards

Subfloor

Joist

Silencing Squeaking Floors & Stairs

Floors and stairs squeak when wooden floor boards or structural beams rub against each other. The X-bridging (wood braces) between the joists can squeak when the floor above flexes under traffic. Floor boards may squeak if they have not been properly nailed to the subfloor. Water pipes or air ducts may also rub against floor joists.

When possible, fix squeaks from underneath the floor or staircase. If the floor or staircase is covered by a finished ceiling, work on squeaks from the top side. With hardwood floors, drive finish nails into the seams between planks to silence squeaking. With floors covered by carpeting or linoleum, fix squeaks when replacing the floorcovering. There also are a number of products designed to fix squeaking floors available at building centers and hardware stores.

Before You Start:

Tools & Materials: hammer, 1-inch wood screws, screwdriver or screwgun, carpenter's glue, hardwood wedges, construction adhesive, caulk gun, wood blocks, flooring nails, nail set.

Three Ways to Silence Squeaking Floors

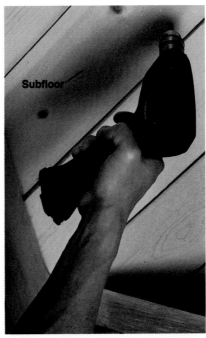

Check pipe hangers, heating ducts and X-bridging for rubbing. Loosen tight pipe hangers and separate wooden bridging to eliminate any rubbing.

Drive wood screws to draw hardwood flooring and subfloor together and stop them from squeaking. Make certain screws are not too long. Use a screwgun to make this overhead task easier.

Cut hardwood wedges and drive the wedges between the joists and subfloor to prevent flexing of the floor.

Three Ways to Silence Squeaking Stairs

Glue wood blocks with construction adhesive underneath stairs to reinforce the joints between treads and risers. After gluing, secure the wood blocks with wood screws.

Cut hardwood wedges and coat them with carpenter's glue. Drive wedges between the treads and risers to tighten the joints and stop squeaks.

Anchor treads to risers by driving flooring nails at opposing angles to prevent loosening. With hardwood, drill pilot holes for nails. Use a nail set to recess nails, then putty nail holes.

Exterior Home Repairs

The goal of most exterior home repairs is to keep your home weather-tight. Leaks in roofing or rain gutters can cause expensive damage to interior ceilings, insulation, furnishings and basements. Window and door frames will rot quickly if they are not periodically recaulked. Open cracks allow insects and pests to enter and cause enormous winter heat loss.

Check the exterior of your home regularly for signs of trouble. Curled and broken shingles and rusted metal flashings and rain gutters cause roof and basement leaks. Check for pools and puddles around the foundation during a rain: these also cause wet-basement problems.

Many exterior repairs require the use of a ladder. Use a ladder as directed by the manufacturer, and never exceed the ladder's weight rating. Note: Never use a ladder when it is raining.

Center your weight on the ladder. Wear clothing such as blue jeans or painters' whites when climbing. Wear rubber-soled, over-the-ankle work shoes for safety and comfort.

Brace ladder before climbing, and read the manufacturer's sticker. Do not use the top shelf or rung as a foot support. Do not overreach when working: move the ladder instead.

Do not climb with your hands full of tools. Assemble all necessary tools and place them in a pail to be hoisted up.

Use cordless tools while climbing on roofs and ladders to avoid the hazard caused by loose tool or extension cords.

Tape scrap carpeting or burlap tightly around the bottom rung of a ladder. Wipe your shoes free of mud or sand to prevent slipping when climbing.

Anchor your ladder. Attach top rung to a short block of wood with rope. Open window, place block inside, and close window.

Fixing a Leaking Roof

Most roof leaks are caused by damaged or worn shingles, or by rusted metal flashings. Flashings line the roof deck wherever there is an interruption in the continuous roofline — such as in valleys, around roof dormers, or whenever skylights, chimneys or vent pipes cut through the roofing.

Ice dams caused by freezing water can back up under the shingles and cause interior water damage.

When you first see signs of ceiling wetness, try to locate the source of the leak and prevent further water damage. Roof leaks are not always found directly above the wet mark on your ceiling. Water can enter the attic and travel far down a rafter before dropping off onto the ceiling below. Wait for dry weather before examining the exterior roofing to find the cause of the leak.

Before You Start:

Tools & Materials: flashlight, hammer, nail, wood block, bucket, awl, pry bar, new shingles, galvanized roofing nails, roofing mastic, caulk gun, sandpaper, fiberglass repair kit, rusty-metal primer, rust-proof paint.

How to Locate a Leak & Minimize Water Damage

1 Check attic for water on rafters and sheathing. Place bucket under dripping water. Trace water to source of leaking, and mark the location.

2 If water flows down toward a wall, nail a small block of wood in the water trickle to direct dripping water into a bucket.

3 Minimize water damage to plaster or wallboard. Locate center of water stain on ceiling. Drive awl or nail into center of stain area to release water into a bucket.

How to Find the Cause of a Roof Leak

Shingles that are broken or curled are likely causes of roof leaks. If you spot a damaged shingle near the suspected location of a leak, replace the shingle (page 132).

Flashings

Metal flashings with rust damage can cause leaks. Flashings seal the roof wherever the roofline is interrupted: around roof vents, chimney, skylight or in valleys where the roofline changes. To correct the problem, repair the flashing (page 133).

Minimize Damage from Ice Dams

Prevent further ice backup by melting a channel through the ice with hot water. This allows water to flow off the roof before it freezes. Or call a professional to thaw and remove ice dams using steam equipment.

Prevent ice dams by improving ventilation and insulation in the attic. Adding ventilation prevents the build-up of heated air which can melt snow on the roof. If the attic is inaccessible, call a professional.

Emergency Roof Repairs

Use a sheet of plywood for an emergency roof cover. Use double-headed nails to temporarily secure the plywood. Patch the nail holes with roof mastic after you remove the nails.

Use plastic sheeting or a tarp to provide emergency cover to a roof after a damaging storm. Hold the edges of the plastic down with nailed strips of lath until roof can be fixed. Patch the nail holes with roof mastic after you remove the nails.

Roof Maintenance Tips

Limbs overhanging roof contribute to moss buildup, and can cause wear to the shingles.

Cut limbs with pruning saw to prevent wear of roofing material, and to increase sunlight. Added sunlight dries roof deck to prevent moss and mildew.

Moss or mildew on a roof deck is caused by too much shade, and by twigs and leaves that block drainage between the shingles. Moss or mildew can cause deterioration in the roofing material.

Power wash the roof deck with a pressure sprayer to eliminate moss and remove twigs and leaves.

Nail zinc strip with sealing roofing nails along the center ridge of shingled roofs to prevent moss buildup. Zinc washes down roof deck during each rain, killing the moss and mildew.

Detect Roof Wear

Curled or cracked shingles caused by years of exposure to the elements are likely to cause roof leaks. Check roof from the ground using binoculars.

Gravel in downspouts or rain gutters indicates that the surface of the shingles is wearing away. Roofing may need to be replaced soon.

How to Replace Shingles

1 Raise the edge of the damaged shingle. Use a slim pry bar to remove nails holding shingle. Remove damaged shingle.

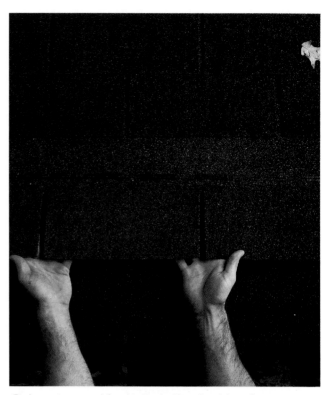

2 Insert new shingle and align it with adjacent shingles. Peel away the liner that covers the adhesive on back of the shingle.

3 Drive galvanized roofing nails near each side and at the top of each slot on the new shingle. Nail heads should be covered by overlapping shingles.

4 Dab roofing mastic over each nail head and press shingles flat. The sun's heat will activate adhesive and seal down the shingle.

How to Repair Flashing

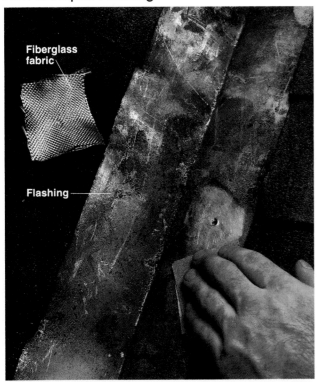

1 Sand metal flashing. Patch rust holes with an automotive fiberglass mending kit, following manufacturer's directions.

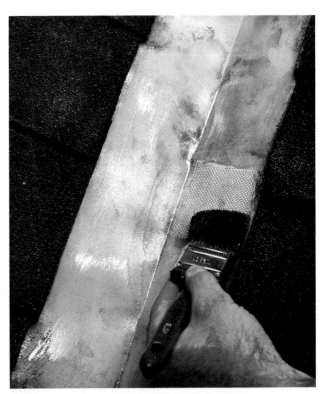

2 Let the fiberglass application harden, then apply several additional coats of resin over the patch, if needed. Let resin set hard.

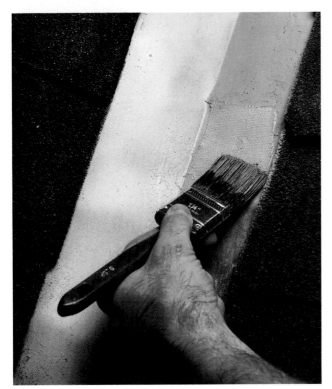

3 Sand patch area and any additional rust spots. Apply a coat of rusty-metal primer to all sanded areas. Let primer dry, then repaint patched flashing with a finish coat of rust-proof paint.

4 Caulk all edges where shingles and flashing meet with a bead of roofing mastic.

Downspout & Gutter Problems & Repairs

Ninety-five percent of all wet basement problems occur because water pools near the foundation. To prevent the problem, fix downspouts and gutters so that rain falling on the roof runs well away from the foundation.

Four Common Problems Caused by Faulty Downspouts & Gutters

Wet basements can cause damage to furnishings, appliances and floorcoverings. Wet basements can usually be traced to roof gutters and downspouts that are plugged, rusted through, or are not diverted away from the house. To correct the problem, fix downspouts and gutters (pages 136, 138), and check the slope of the earth around the foundation (page 137).

Peeling paint on basement walls is caused by moisture in the wall behind the paint. This is usually caused by water seeping through the wall from the outside. To correct the problem, fix the downspouts and gutters (pages 136, 138), and check the slope of the earth around the foundation (page 137).

After checking and fixing downspouts and gutters, check the soil grade around the house, and, if necessary, create a slight downhill slope away from the walls.

Before You Start:

Tools & Materials: trowel, garden hose, mesh leaf guard, carpenter's level, sandpaper or paint scraper, replacement gutter section, roof mastic, fiberglass repair kit, rusty-metal primer, rust-proof paint, hacksaw, ground pipe extension.

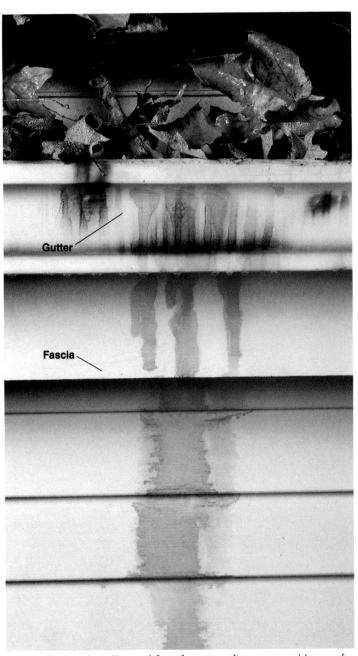

Stained walls and fascias are often caused by roof gutters that leak or overflow. Gutters overflow if they are plugged with leaves and debris. To correct the problem, fix downspouts and gutters (pages 136, 138), and check the slope of the earth around the foundation (page 137).

Puddles on walkways will cause the concrete to deteriorate. Icy sidewalks are dangerous, and wherever dripping water causes ice on sidewalks, there is also a danger of falling icicles. To correct the problem, fix downspouts and gutters (pages 136, 138), check the slope of the slab (page 137), and repair and seal concrete (pages 146-147).

Gutter

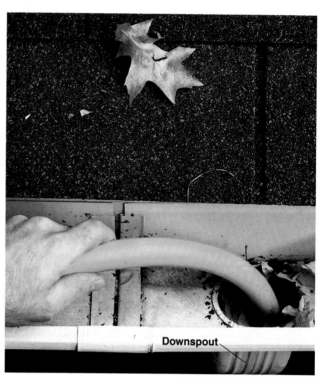

Downspout

1 Clean leaves, twigs and other material out of rain gutters using a trowel. Debris in gutters can hold moisture and cause galvanized gutters to rust.

2 Flush out the debris by inserting a garden hose into the downspout, and turning on the water. Check for rust in gutters, and repair any holes (page 138).

Leaf guard

Check slope of gutters with a level. Gutters should angle toward downspouts. Water that stands in gutters can cause metal to rust.

Shield gutters with a mesh leaf guard to prevent clogs in the downspouts. Leaves are washed over gutters during rain.

How to Check & Correct a Foundation Grade

1 Tape a carpenter's level to a straight 8-foot-long 2 × 4 board, and check the grade around the house. If the earth around the foundation is level, standing water can seep into the basement.

2 Add soil around the foundation to increase the grade away from the foundation. Rake the soil smooth, and recheck the slope.

Ground pipe

3 For proper grade, the outside end of the 2 × 4 should be at least 6" above the ground when the 2 × 4 is level. Add a ground pipe to deliver water at least 6 to 8 feet from the foundation (page 139). Plant grass right up to the foundation to help shed water.

Concrete slabs such as walks or patios should slope away from the house. If slab is level or slopes toward foundation, consider having it raised by "mud-jacking." Look under Concrete Contractors in your Yellow Pages for a contractor who offers this service.

How to Repair a Leaking Gutter

1 Scrape away any peeling paint and rust, using sandpaper or scraper. Patch holes with a section of matching gutter. Use a fiberglass repair kit to patch other rusty areas.

2 Cut a section of matching gutter to cover gutter areas that are rusted through. Apply roof mastic to patch area, then press patch firmly in place.

3 For other rusty areas, brush fiberglass resin on metal. Cover resin with fiberglass fabric cut to fit gutter. Let resin harden slightly, then brush on more. Let resin dry overnight.

4 Coat all repair areas with a rusty-metal primer. Let primer dry, then repaint patched gutters with finish coat of rust-proof paint.

How to Extend Downspouts

1 Water pooling near foundation can cause a wet basement. Begin by checking the slope of the foundation grade (page 137).

2 Use a hacksaw to cut a section of downspout that is 6 to 8 feet long.

3 Attach the pipe to the downspout with a galvanized elbow.

4 Place a splash block at the end of the ground pipe to disperse water onto the lawn.

Filling Cracks & Holes

Caulks block air movement and help conserve energy. They also prevent water, dirt, and pests from entering.

A wide variety of modern caulks are available to fill cracks and holes in wood, masonry, concrete, and blacktop. Fill large gaps in foundations and siding with fiberglass insulation to form a base for the caulk. Large gaps in masonry should be filled with new mortar. There are also specialty patching products available at building centers and hardware stores.

Before You Start:

Tools & Materials: tube caulks, utility knife, caulk gun, fiberglass insulation, smoothing tool (plastic spoon or flat stick), masonry chisel, ball peen hammer, mortar, pointed trowel, joint tool, muriatic acid.

Tip: Keep a bowl of cold water handy and dip the smoothing tool (or your fingertip) to avoid smearing latex caulk. Clean up butyl or oil-base caulks with mineral spirits.

Types of caulk include (clockwise from top left): peel-and-stick caulk, roofing mastic, butyl-base caulk, acrylic latex caulk, butyl driveway patcher, latex masonry patcher, clear weatherproofing caulk.

How to Use a Caulk Gun

1 Cut off tip of caulk tube to the desired bead size. Some caulk tubes have trimming guides on the tip.

2 Insert a long nail to break seal on tube. Insert tube into caulk gun and push the plunger against the base of caulk tube.

3 Hold the gun at an angle and squeeze trigger evenly while caulking. Draw tip of caulk tube steadily to apply an even bead.

4 Set caulk tube on scrap wood, and pull plunger back to avoid drips. Wipe excess caulk from tip. Cover tip to prevent the tube from drying out.

Dip a flat stick in water and use it to smooth a latex caulk bead in locations where appearance is important.

A wet finger can also be used to smooth a latex or silicone caulk bead. Keep water handy to rinse caulk and moisten finger.

Tips for Sealing Holes & Cracks in Exterior Walls

Caulk windows and doors with a good-quality latex or silicone caulk. Caulking prevents moisture from rotting the wood, and reduces heat loss.

Caulk around wires and pipes entering the house. Remove old, cracked caulk before applying new, colored caulk that matches siding.

Caulk mud sill, the horizontal wooden plate where the house rests on the foundation. This should be periodically recaulked to prevent heat loss.

Stuff fiberglass insulation into large holes and cracks to provide a base for the caulk. Fiberglass also insulates.

Caulk under shingles with a good-quality roof mastic.

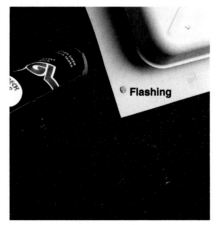

Caulk roof flashings around chimneys, vents and skylights with roof mastic to protect against water entry.

Coat nailheads with roof mastic to prevent leaks after replacing roof shingles.

How to Fill Masonry Cracks

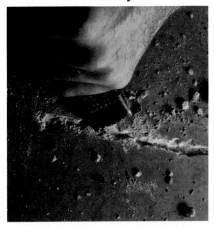

1 Remove loose masonry with a masonry chisel and wire brush. Clean surfaces with brush or hand vacuum.

2 Use a caulk gun to apply masonry patch to crack. Latex masonry fillers are easy to apply and clean up.

3 Smooth the masonry caulk with a putty knife, trowel, or with a wooden dowel.

How to Replace Mortar

1 Chip out loose mortar with a masonry chisel and ball peen hammer. Clean cracks with a wire brush or hand vacuum.

2 Mix fresh mortar and apply to cracks with a pointed trowel.

3 Smooth mortar with a smoothing tool or round wooden dowel. Let mortar dry overnight.

4 Clean brick face with a brush and a 5% muriatic acid solution, available at home centers. Wear protective clothes when working with acid.

Concrete Repairs

Concrete can be broken or chipped, stained by rust or oil, or cracked by the effects of water — the chief enemy of concrete. Keep the concrete slab well sealed, and repair soil erosion around the slab to prevent water from getting underneath.

Pop-ups are conical holes in concrete, caused by expansion of a rock chip at the base of the hole.

Cracks in concrete are caused by expansion and contraction of the slab. This is caused by temperature changes, or by water washing away the gravel base.

Chipped corners on steps are usually caused by a blow with a heavy object.

Stains on concrete can occur when the surface is not sealed. Seal concrete with a clear masonry

sealer once each year for maximum protection against staining and water damage.

Before You Start:

Tools & Materials: muriatic acid, rubber gloves, eye protection, trisodium phosphate (TSP), squeegee/broom or paint roller, masonry chisel, ball peen hammer, powdered concrete patcher with bonding liquid, trowel, caulk-type concrete patcher.

Tip: Repair concrete when temperature is 50° to 80°F and winds are light. Concrete will not set properly if it dries too fast, or if it freezes while wet.

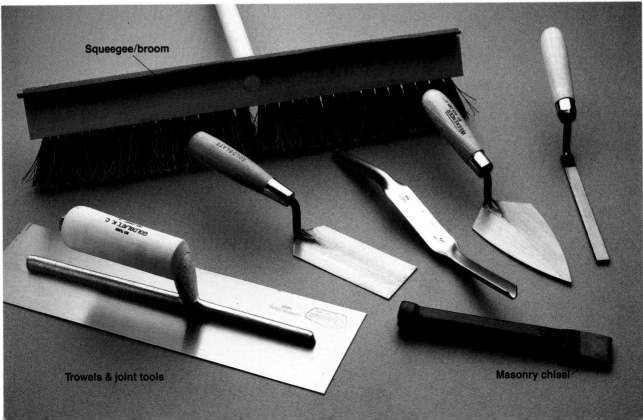

Squeegee/broom

Trowels & joint tools

Masonry chisel

How to Clean & Seal Concrete

1 Clean concrete with brush and a 5% solution of muriatic acid, available at home centers. Wear gloves and protective clothes when working with acid.

2 Flush the surface with TSP (tri-sodium phosphate) solution, then rinse with hose or high-pressure power washer.

3 Apply concrete sealer with a paint roller, squeegee or garden sprayer.

How to Repair Chipped Concrete Steps

1 Clean chipped concrete with a wire brush. Brush patch area with latex bonding liquid.

2 Mix concrete patcher with water, then stir in bonding liquid, as directed by manufacturer. Apply to patch area with flexible knife or trowel.

3 Tape scrap lumber pieces around corner of step, as shown, to hold the patch until it hardens.

How to Patch Pop-ups & Cracks in Concrete

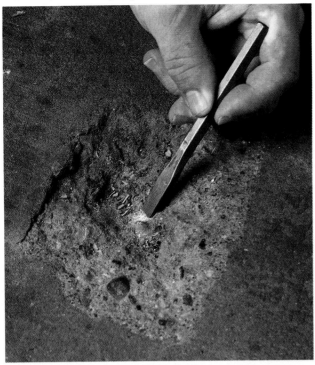

1 Chip out rocks at bottom of pop-up hole with a masonry chisel and hammer. Wear goggles to avoid eye injury.

2 Remove dirt and debris from hole with a shop vacuum. If hole contains oil or grease, wash with a detergent, then rinse with water.

3 Coat the edges of the hole with a latex bonding liquid. Mix concrete with water, then stir in bonding liquid. Pour in the mixture, and smooth with a flexible knife or trowel.

Cracks between a concrete walk and foundation can cause a wet basement. Repair cracks with caulk-type concrete patcher.

Asphalt Care & Repair

Asphalt blacktop driveways and walks can be damaged by impact or by water penetration. Water running under blacktop from the side or through cracks will undermine the gravel base that cushions the slab. To repair asphalt and prevent serious damage, fill holes and cracks with asphalt patcher, seal the surface, and fill washouts along the slab edge to prevent water from entering.

Before You Start:

Tools & Materials: garden hose, vacuum, heat gun, trowel, asphalt cleaner, caulk gun, asphalt patcher, putty knife, asphalt sealer, squeegee/broom.

Tip: Wait for a warm, sunny day to seal asphalt.

How to Patch Holes in Asphalt

1 Remove dirt and debris from hole with a shop vacuum. Flush the hole with a garden hose and spray nozzle.

2 Pour asphalt patching material into the hole. Warm patch material with heat gun. Level and smooth the patch with a trowel.

3 Tamp patching material so it is firmly packed in hole. Firm, smooth patches prevent future water damage.

How to Seal an Asphalt Drive

1 Fill any holes in slab (page opposite). Clean slab with asphalt-cleaning product to remove oil and dirt from surface. Rinse slab with hose or power washer.

2 Patch cracks in asphalt using caulk gun and a tube of asphalt patcher. Large cracks may need several applications.

3 Spread and smooth the patch material using a putty knife. Dip scraper in cold water or mineral spirits to prevent the patcher from sticking to scraper.

4 Pour a pool of sealer on the slab and spread it following manufacturer's directions. Too thick a layer will not cure properly. It is better to apply two coats.

5 Allow sealer to cure well before driving or walking on it. Block drive with sawhorses or rope and ladders to prevent traffic during the drying period.

Inspect hidden areas regularly for signs of rotted or damaged wood. Apply a fresh coat of finish yearly.

Maintaining a Deck

Inspect your deck once each year. Replace loose or rusting hardware or fasteners, and apply fresh finish to prevent water damage.

Look carefully for areas that show signs of damage. Replace or reinforce damaged wood as soon as possible.

Restore an older, weathered deck to the original wood color with a deck-brightening solution. Brighteners are available at any home improvement store.

Everything You Need:

Tools: flashlight, awl or screwdriver, screwgun, putty knife, scrub brush, rubber gloves, eye protection, pressure sprayer.

Materials: 2½" corrosion-resistant deck screws, deck brightener.

Tips for Maintaining an Older Deck

Use an awl or screwdriver to check deck for soft, rotted wood. Replace or reinforce damaged wood.

How to Renew a Deck

1 Mix deck-brightening solution as directed by manufacturer. Apply solution with pressure sprayer. Let solution set for 10 minutes.

Clean debris from cracks between decking boards with a putty knife. Debris traps moisture, and can cause wood to rot.

Drive new fasteners to secure loose decking to joists. If using the old nail or screw holes, new fasteners should be slightly longer than the originals.

2 Scrub deck thoroughly with a stiff scrub brush. Wear rubber gloves and eye protection.

3 Rinse deck with clear water. If necessary, apply a second coat of brightener to extremely dirty or stained areas. Rinse and let dry. Apply a fresh coat of sealer or stain.

Repairing a Deck

Replace or reinforce damaged deck wood as soon as possible. Wood rot can spread and weaken solid wood.

After replacing or reinforcing the rotted wood, clean the entire deck and apply a fresh coat of clear sealer-preservative or staining sealer. Apply a fresh coat of finish each year to prevent future water damage.

Everything You Need:

Tools: cat's paw or flat pry bar, screwgun, awl or screwdriver, hammer, chisel, eye protection, pressure-sprayer, circular saw, scrub brush, paint brush, hydraulic jack, drill or hammer drill, ⅝" masonry bit, level, ratchet wrench.

Materials: sealer-preservative or staining sealer, galvanized nails (6d, 10d), deck lumber, baking soda, corrosion-resistant deck screws, ⅝" masonry anchor, ⅜" lag screw.

Supplies: rubber gloves, bucket, concrete block, scrap plywood.

How to Repair Damaged Decking & Joists

1 Remove nails or screws from the damaged decking board, using a cat's paw or screwgun. Remove the damaged board.

4 Apply a thick coat of sealer-preservative to damaged joist. Let dry, then apply a second coat of sealer. Cut a reinforcing joist (sister joist) from pressure-treated lumber.

5 Treat all sides of sister joist with clear sealer-preservative, and let dry. Position sister joist tightly against the damaged joist, and attach with 10d nails driven every 2 feet.

2 Inspect the underlying joists for signs of rotted wood. Joists with discolored, soft areas should be repaired and reinforced.

3 Use a hammer and chisel to remove any rotted portions of joist.

6 Attach sister joist to ledger and header joist by toenailing with 10d nails. Cut replacement decking boards from matching lumber, using a circular saw.

7 If the existing decking is gray, "weather" the new decking by scrubbing with a solution made from 1 cup baking soda and 1 gallon warm water. Rinse and let dry.

(continued next page)

How to Repair Damaged Decking & Joists (continued)

8 Apply a coat of sealer-preservative or staining sealer to all sides of the new decking board.

9 Position the new decking and attach to joists with galvanized deck screws or nails. Make sure space between boards matches that of existing decking.

How to Replace a Post on an Older Deck

1 Build a support, using plywood scraps, a concrete block, and a hydraulic jack. Place 1½" layer of plywood between head of jack and beam. Apply just enough pressure to lift the beam slightly.

Anchor pad

2 Remove the nails or lag screws holding the damaged post to the anchor pad and to the beam. Remove the damaged post and the wood anchor pad on the concrete pier.

3 Drill a hole in the middle of the concrete pier, using a hammer drill and a ⅝" masonry bit. Insert ⅝" masonry anchor into hole.

4 Position galvanized post anchor on pier block, and thread a ⅜" lag screw with washer through the hole in the anchor and into the masonry anchor. Tighten the screw with a ratchet wrench.

5 Cut new post from pressure-treated lumber, and treat cut ends with sealer-preservative. Position post and make sure it is plumb.

6 Attach the bottom of the post to the post anchor, using 6d galvanized nails. Attach the post to the beam by redriving the lag screws, using a ratchet wrench. Release the pressure on the jack and remove the support.

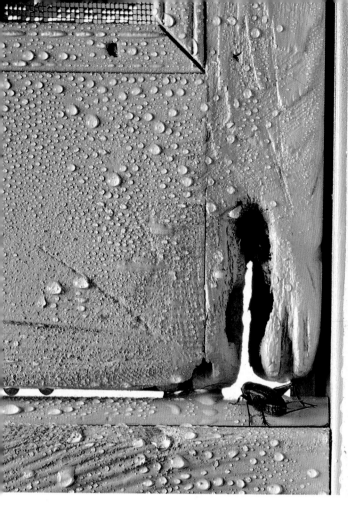

Preserving & Repairing Wood

Even durable woods like redwood or cedar benefit from a protective coat of sealer, stain or paint. Periodically inspect exterior doors, window sashes and decks so that rot or insect damage can be stopped before it becomes widespread. Seal joints around windows and doors with caulk to block entry by moisture or insects.

To repair existing wood damage, use one of the epoxy wood fillers available. Wood fillers can be molded and shaped easily, and they readily accept paint or stain.

Before You Start:
Tools & Materials: chisel, eye protection, wood filler, putty knives, sander, wood strips, tacks, tack hammer.

Protect wood exposed to weather with a clear or pigmented sealer. Treat wood yearly for best protection.

Repair damaged or rotted wood with epoxy wood filler (page opposite).

How to Repair Damaged Wood

1 Remove damaged wood with a chisel or utility knife. Wear eye protection while chiseling wood.

2 Build simple wooden forms as needed to establish repair boundaries. Coat forms with wax or oil so filler will not adhere to them.

3 Mix and apply wood filler according to directions. Shape repair area with putty knife or trowel to match existing contours. Let filler harden completely.

4 Remove forms. Sand hardened filler lightly — oversanding closes filler pores and makes staining difficult. Paint or stain the wood to match the existing finish.

Index